The Homeric Hymns

The
Johns Hopkins
University Press,
Baltimore and
London

*Translation,
Introduction, and
Notes*

THE HOMERIC HYMNS

Apostolos N. Athanassakis

Copyright © 1976 by The Johns Hopkins University Press
Johns Hopkins Paperbacks edition, 1976
All rights reserved
Printed in the United States of America on acid-free paper

20 19 18 17 16

The Johns Hopkins University Press
2715 North Charles Street
Baltimore, Maryland 21218-4363
www.press.jhu.edu

Library of Congress Cataloging in Publication Data

Homerus.
   The Homeric Hymns

   Includes bibliographical references.
   I. Athanassakis, Apostolos N.   II. Title
PA4025.H8A8   1976   883.01   75–40305
ISBN 0-8018-1792-7 (pbk.)

A catalog record for this book is available from the British Library.

Antidôron to John and Kirsten

Contents

POETRY is untranslatable, and the present translation does not claim to be poetry. My rendition is a line-by-line English version of the original Greek. I have aimed for accuracy rather than for poetic effect, although, wherever I could, I tried to preserve for the reader the vigor and beauty of the original. I did not modernize traditional renditions of certain epithets and phrases, and I refused to lengthen or truncate lines for metrical or symmetrical purposes. I made an effort to keep to an iambic flow, but here again I preferred to violate this flow rather than to sacrifice accuracy. The reason for a verse translation rather than a prose translation is simple: the reader can refer to lines more easily, and, should he be interested in comparing this rendition with the Greek text, he will find it easier to do so. In addition to this, a straight prose translation would bear even less resemblance to the original.

The Homeric Hymns have been neglected both in antiquity and in modern times. We call them Homeric, not because we believe that Homer composed them but merely because for a long time the ancients thought that Homer did compose them and, therefore, they referred to them as Homeric. So pious was the attitude of the ancients toward Homer that, once the Alexandrians discarded the idea of Homeric authorship, the integrity and worth of the hymns came under suspicion. It is my sincere hope that the student of ancient Greek religion, mythology, and literature will not fail to see in the hymns a treasure-trove of valuable information and charming poetry.

I wish to apologize to the readers for failing to be absolutely consistent in spelling Greek names. Wherever possible, I have tried simply to transliterate the Greek name in order to preserve its Hellenic character. In some cases I gave in to the established Latinate or Anglicized form. In the notes I employed the macron sparingly to indicate vowel length and to avoid grossly infelicitous mispronunciation (e.g., Dymê, Dikê, Samê to avoid confusion with "dime," "dike," "same," etc.).

References to ancient authors are usually from the *Oxford Classical Texts* (*OCT*). For the lyrical poets I have referred the reader to West (*Iambi et Elegi Graeci,* ed. M. S. West, Oxford, 1972), to the *PML* (*Poetae Melici Graeci,* ed. Denys Page, Oxford, 1962), and to *LP* (*Poetarum Lesbiorum Fragmenta,* ed., Edgar Lobel and Denys Page, Oxford, 1955). *Loeb,* of course, refers to the three volumes of the *Lyra Graeca* subseries of the *Loeb Classical Library* of which J. M. Edmonds is the translator. Bergk in parenthesis stands for Theodor Bergk's *Poetae Lyrici Graeci.* Because I cannot expect all readers to be familiar with abbreviations used by classicists, I should also clarify the following:

IG	Inscriptiones Graecae
CIG	Corpus Inscriptionum Graecarum
BCH	Bulletin de Correspondence Hellénique
Thuc.	Thucydides
Paus.	Pausanias
Arist.	Aristophanes

Throughout the preparation of the translation and the notes, I have had numerous occasions to make use of the learned commentary to the hymns by T. W. Allen, W. R. Halliday, E. E. Sikes (2d. ed., Oxford, 1936). It goes without saying that my debt to this impressive repository of information about the hymns should be acknowledged.

I gratefully acknowledge my debt to Professors Lloyd W. Daly and H. D. F. Kitto for their wise comments and suggested corrections. I wish to thank colleagues and graduate students of the Classics Department at the University of California at Santa Barbara to whom I ran for help when I could not find the right word. My colleagues Purcell Weaver and Dr. Birger Pearson, as well as Richard Panofsky of the English Department, are to be thanked for helping me improve the rendition of the Hymn to Apollon. Karen Jaehne, M.A. (Classics), and Mary Husung deserve my gratitude for assisting me in proofreading and verifying references. Finally, my friend and fellow classicist, David Creeth, should receive due credit for being no less tolerant of infelicitous expression than the unforgettable Caterpillar of *Alice in Wonderland.* I need not add that the onus of the remaining errors sits squarely on my shoulders.

University of California
at Santa Barbara

Preface

THE HOMERIC HYMNS have come down to us in a text that has been established quite securely through collation of thirty manuscripts that are scattered in various European libraries (the list is to be found both in the *OCT* edition of the hymns and, in more detailed fashion, in the Allen-Halliday-Sikes commentary, pp. xi-xvii). That Greece should possess only one manuscript—the so-called *Athous* in the monastery of Vatopedi on Mt. Athos—is an indication both of the vicissitudes of Greek history and of the rapacity of conqueror and unscrupulous visitor. Of the existing thirty-one manuscripts the best one is the *Mosquensis* (M). It is a late thirteenth or early fourteenth-century manuscript, which was discovered in the library of the Synod at Moscow in 1777. It now is in the possession of the University Library at Leiden. The hymns were included along with the *Iliad* and the *Odyssey* in the *editio princeps* of the Homerica, which was done in Florence by Demetrios Chalcocondyles in the year 1488.

Classical and even Hellenistic antiquity treated the Homeric Hymns with a considerable measure of indifference. This is rather difficult to understand, especially since they were ascribed to Homer. From the fifth century we have a sole quotation of lines 146-50 and 165-72 of the *Hymn to Apollon* in Thucydides 3.104. The third-century scholar Antigonos of Karystos (fl. 240 B.C.) quotes one line from the *Hymn to Hermes* (51), in order to support the opinion that the guts of ewes, but not of rams, are "euphonic", that is, resonant enough to be used as lyre strings. To Diodorus Siculus (1st c. B.C.), we owe lines 1-9 of Hymn 1 to Dionysos. Diodorus refers to the hymns three times and in a manner that leaves it unclear whether he is quoting from the original (Diodorus Siculus 1.15.7; 3.66.3; 4.2.4). The only other first-century B.C. author to refer to the hymns is Philodemus in his *Peri Eusebeias;* the reference is to a word in line 440 of the *Hymn to Demeter.* In the second century A.D. the references are equally scarce. Pausanias merely refers to the *Hymn to Demeter* twice (1.38.3; one of the references in this passage must be to a line not contained in the text as we now have it). He excerpts three lines (417, 418, 420) from the same hymn (4.30.3), and in a third reference calls upon the *Hymn to Apollon* to prove that Homer names the city below

Delphi, Krisa in both the *Iliad* and in the hymn (10.37.4). Athenaeus is the first writer to use a quotation from the hymns (lines 514–16 from *Hymn to Apollon,* found in Athenaeus 223) and to call into question Homer's authorship. He implies that the *Hymn to Apollon* may have been written by one of the Homeridae. From the same century we have a quotation by the rhetor Aelius Aristides of lines 169–71 of the *Hymn to Apollon* (2, p. 559 in Dindorf's edition).

Except for a few scattered references, chiefly by later scholiasts and antiquarians, the hymns seem to have suffered from a nearly universal literary conspiracy of silence. That we should have only scant evidence of the influence of the hymns on classical authors is not so difficult to understand, but that the Alexandrian literateurs and antiquarians should ignore this important body of literature we may benignly attribute to literary orthodoxy and exclusive *prosopolatry.* It is interesting that no less a writer than Thucydides obviously accepted the tradition that ascribed the hymns to Homer, but the Alexandrian grammarians and critics made up their minds that the hymns had not been composed by the poet of the *Iliad* and the *Odyssey*

and that, therefore, they did not deserve the attention lavished on Homer. There is no evidence that the Romans took notice of the hymns, and the Byzantines, obviously following the verdict of the Alexandrians, consigned them to the limbo of condescending indifference. In modern times scholars have recognized the importance of the hymns, but students of the classics frequently bypass them for the study of the Homeric epics, and the educated public is hardly aware of their existence.

The tradition to which the Homeric Hymns belong may not be less pristine than that of the two great Homeric epics, which have so completely overshadowed them to the present day. Greek tradition has preserved the names of hymnists such as Orpheus, Linos, and Mousaios, who may have preceded

Introduction

Homer by hundreds of years. The term *hymnos,* "hymn", is generic and denotes a type of devotional song sung in honor of a god or goddess, usually at a contest held as part of a religious festival or of some other solemn occasion with religious overtones. The Homeric Hymns are distinguished from other hymnic poetry both by their meter, the dactylic hexameter, and by the formulae that the poet employs at the beginning and at the end of each poem. The ancients called these poems hymns and specifically, *prooimia,* preludes, that is, because the poets used them as warm-up pieces for the singing or recitation of longer portions of the Homeric epics. Of the extant Homeric Hymns four, to Demeter, Apollon, Hermes, and Aphrodite, are long enough to have been recited or sung independently. However, we cannot be sure that they too were not used as preludes to even more ambitious compositions. Not all the hymns seem equally devotional. The hymns to Hermes and Aphrodite, for example, even contain comic elements, which, from our point of view, are hardly consonant with the spirit of piety that must permeate a religious occasion. Here, however, we must be careful not to project our own ideas of religious propriety onto

those of the ancient Greeks, whose gods laughed and danced, whereas ours do not.

The *Hymn to Apollon* is the only one for which we have the name of the composer and what appears to be a false date. About the other hymns we do not know who composed them or when and where they were composed. Yet, internal evidence shows that some of them come from the eighth and seventh centuries, others from the sixth and fifth, and a very few are later, though not necessarily Hellenistic. We are therefore dealing with literary documents of great antiquity. Unfortunately, the ancients did not leave us learned commentaries to the hymns. Thus we are tantalized by unexplained allusions and enigmatic statements. But even so the hymns have so much to tell us about Greek religion and mythology. There is no other single document, for example, which teaches us as much about Demeter and Apollon as the two long hymns to these gods. But a utilitarian view of the hymns is a very limited and unfair one. After all, we are dealing with poems and not with annalistic accounts. Two of the shorter hymns (7, 19) and the four longer ones (2, 3, 4, 5) are poems of great beauty and skill. The modern reader who is not familiar with epic technique may be taken aback by a pace that can be leisurely enough to digress exactly where we feel the action must go on and abruptly vigorous enough to begin totally *in medias res* (7). Surely, the modern reader will weary of the list of places over which Apollon "ruled" (*Hymn to Apollon* 25-46), but he must be reminded that to the ancients it was important that due recognition be given to each of these places. Who can deny that poetic genius is at work in the *Hymn to Demeter* and in the incomparably subtle mixture of humor, seduction, and piety in the longer *Hymn to Aphrodite*? But the poets of the hymns do not need advocates or highly literate and fastidious readers. They need listeners who love good poetry for its own sake and who can believe that, if Jesus of Nazareth can resurrect the dead and turn water to wine, Apollon of Delphi can change into a dolphin and, much like St. George, slay the dragon if he so wishes.

And to add a footnote to this discussion, Professor Elroy Bundy in his long and learned essay "Quarrel between Kallimachos and Apollonios" (*California Studies in Classical Antiquity*, vol. 5, 1972, pp. 39-94, and especially pp. 49-55)

has convincingly argued that the *chaire* of the rhapsodic *envoi* is more than just "hail" or "farewell." However, even if the meaning is more propitiatory than salutatory, the search for equivalents closer to the literal meaning, "be glad," "rejoice," is bound to be fruitless, as those who know the literal meaning of "good-bye" or "hail" will readily agree. It is only for lack of better approximations that I have retained the traditional translations. After all, *chaire* (now usually *chairete*) may mean hello or good-bye in Greece today, but it may also mean hail, as it does in the Greek national anthem. It all depends on the occasion and the context.

The Homeric Hymns

1. FRAGMENTS OF THE HYMN TO DIONYSOS
(Verses 1–9 are preserved by Diodorus Siculus 3.66.3)

1   Some, O divine Eiraphiotes, say that Drakanon was your birthplace,
    but others claim it was at the wind-swept island of Ikaros, others at Naxos,
    and others by the deep-eddying river Alpheios
    that Semele conceived and bore you to Zeus who delights in thunder;
5   And, O lord, some liars say you were born
    at Thebes when in truth the father of gods and men
    gave birth to you and kept you well out of the sight of men and of white-armed Hera.
    There is a certain Nysa, a lofty mountain overgrown with trees,
    far from Phoinike and near the flowing stream of the Aigyptos.
               (Here begins folium 31 of codex M):
10 "... And for her they will set up many statues in temples.
    As he cut you into three pieces, in triennial feasts
    men shall always sacrifice to you unblemished hecatombs."
    So said Kronion and nodded with his dark brows,
    and the lord's ambrosial mane streamed down
15 from his immortal head and great Olympos was shaken.
    Thus spoke Zeus the counselor and gave orders with nodding head.
    Eiraphiotes, woman-maddener, be propitious to us singers
    who start and finish our song with you; there is no way
    for the one who forgets you to remember his song.
20 So hail, Dionysos Eiraphiotes,
    and your mother, Semele, whom they call Thyone.

2. TO DEMETER

1   I begin to sing of lovely-haired Demeter, the goddess august,
    of her and her slender-ankled daughter whom Zeus,
    far-seeing and loud-thundering, gave to Aidoneus to abduct.
    Away from her mother of the golden sword and the splendid fruit
5   she played with the full-bosomed daughters of Okeanos,
    gathering flowers, roses, crocuses, and beautiful violets

1

all over a soft meadow; irises, too, and hyacinths she picked,
and narcissus, which Gaia, pleasing the All-receiver,
made blossom there, by the will of Zeus, for a girl with a flower's beauty.
10 A lure it was, wondrous and radiant, and a marvel to be seen
by immortal gods and mortal men.
A hundred stems of sweet-smelling blossoms
grew from its roots. The wide sky above
and the whole earth and the briny swell of the sea laughed.
15 She was dazzled and reached out with both hands at once
to take the pretty bauble; Earth with its wide roads gaped
and then over the Nysian field the lord and All-receiver,
the many-named son of Kronos, sprang out upon her with his immortal horses.
Against her will he seized her and on his golden chariot
20 carried her away as she wailed; and she raised a shrill cry,
calling upon father Kronides, the highest and the best.
None of the immortals or of mortal men heard
her voice, not even the olive-trees bearing splendid fruit.
Only the gentle-tempered daughter of Persaios,
25 Hekate of the shining headband, heard from her cave,
and lord Helios, the splendid son of Hyperion, heard
the maiden calling father Kronides; he sat
apart from the gods away in the temple of prayers,
accepting beautiful sacrifices from mortal men.
30 By Zeus' counsels, his brother, the All-receiver
and Ruler of Many, Kronos' son of many names,
was carrying her away with his immortal horses, against her will.
So while the goddess looked upon the earth and the starry sky
and the swift-flowing sea teeming with fish
35 and the rays of the sun and still hoped to see
her loving mother and the races of gods immortal,
hope charmed her great mind, despite her grief.
The peaks of the mountains and the depths of the sea resounded
with her immortal voice, and her mighty mother heard her.
40 A sharp pain gripped her heart, and she tore
the headband round her divine hair with her own hands.
From both of her shoulders she cast down her dark veil

and rushed like a bird over the nourishing land and the sea,
searching; but none of the gods or mortal men
45 wanted to tell her the truth and none
of the birds of omen came to her as truthful messenger.
For nine days then all over the earth mighty Deo
roamed about with bright torches in her hands,
and in her sorrow never tasted ambrosia
50 or nectar sweet to drink, and never bathed her skin.
But when the tenth light-bringing Dawn came to her,
Hekate carrying a light in her hands, met her,
and with loud voice spoke to her and told her the news:
"Mighty Demeter, bringer of seasons and splendid gifts,
55 which of the heavenly gods or of mortal men
seized Persephone and pierced with sorrow your dear heart?
For I heard a voice but did not see with my eyes
who it was; I am quickly telling you the whole truth."
Thus spoke Hekate. And to her the daughter of lovely-haired Rhea
60 answered not a word, but with her she sped away
swiftly, holding the bright torches in her hands.
They came to Helios, watcher of gods and men,
and stood near his horses, and the illustrious goddess made a plea:
"Helios, do have respect for me as a goddess, if I ever
65 cheered your heart and soul by word or deed.
Through the barren ether I heard the shrieking voice
of my daughter famous for her beauty, a sweet flower at birth,
as if she were being overcome by force, but I saw nothing.
And since you do gaze down upon the whole earth
70 and sea and cast your rays through the bright ether,
tell me truly if you have seen anywhere
what god or even mortal man in my absence
seized by force my dear child and went away."
Thus she spoke and Hyperionides gave her an answer:
75 "Lady Demeter, daughter of lovely-haired Rhea,
you shall know; for I greatly reverence and pity you
in your grief for your slender-ankled child; no other immortal
is to be blamed save cloud-gathering Zeus

3

who gave her to Hades, his own brother, to become
80 his buxom bride. He seized her and with his horses
carried her crying loud down to misty darkness.
But, Goddess, stop your great wailing; you mustn't give
yourself to grief so great and fruitless. Not an unseemly
bridegroom among immortals is Aidoneus, Lord of Many,
85 your own brother from the same seed; to his share fell
honor when in the beginning a triple division was made,
and he dwells among those over whom his lot made him lord."
With these words, he called upon his horses, and at his command
speedily, like long-winged birds, they drew the swift chariot,
90 as a pain more awful and savage reached Demeter's soul.
Afterwards, angered with Kronion, lord of black clouds,
she withdrew from the assembly of the gods and from lofty Olympos
and went through the cities of men and the wealth of their labors,
tearing at her fair form for a long time; no man
95 or deep-girded woman looking at her knew who she was
before she reached the house of prudent Keleos,
who then was lord of Eleusis, a town rich in sacrifices.
Grieving in her dear heart, she sat near the road,
at Parthenion, the well from which the citizens drew water,
100 in the shade of a bushy olive-tree which grew above it.
She looked like an old woman born a long time ago
and barred from childbearing and the gifts of wreath-loving Aphrodite,
even as are nurses for the children of law-tending
kings and keepers of the storerooms in their bustling mansions.
105 The daughters of Keleos Eleusinides saw her
as they were coming to fetch easily-drawn water
in copper vessels to their father's dear halls,
four of them in their maidenly bloom, like goddesses,
Kallidike, Kleisidike and Demo the lovely,
110 and Kallithoe, who was the eldest of them all.
They did not know who she was; it is hard for mortals to see divinity.
Standing near they addressed her with winged words:
"Old woman, whence and from what older generation do you come?
Why have you wandered away from the city and not approached

4

115   a house; there in the shadowy halls live
women of your age and even younger ones
who will treat you kindly in both word and deed."
After these words, the mighty goddess answered:
"Dear children, whoever of ladylike women you are,
120   I greet you and will explain; indeed it is fitting
to tell you the truth, since you are asking.
Dos is the name which my mighty mother gave me.   *Dos = dosis = giving*
And now from Crete on the broad back of the sea
I came unwillingly; marauding men by brute force
125   carried me off against my will, and later
they landed their swift ship at Thorikos, where the women
came out in a body and the men themselves
prepared a meal by the stern-cables of the ship.
But my heart had no desire for the evening's sweet meal;
130   I eluded them and, rushing through the black land,
I fled my reckless masters, so that they might not enjoy
the benefit of my price, since, like thieves, they carried me across the sea.
So I have wandered to this place and know not at all
what land this is and what men live in it.
135   But may all who dwell in the Olympian halls
grant you men to wed and children to bear
as your parents wish; and now have mercy on me, maidens
and, dear children, kindly let me go to someone's house,
a man's and a woman's, to work for them
140   in such tasks as befit a woman past her prime.
I shall be a good nurse to a new-born child,
holding him in my arms; I shall take care of the house,
and make the master's bed in the innermost part
of the well-built chamber and mind his wife's work."
145   So said the goddess, and forthwith Kallidike, still a pure virgin
and the most beautiful of Keleos' daughters, replied:
"Good mother, men must take the gifts of the gods
even when they bring them pain, since gods are truly much stronger.
I shall advise you clearly and give you the names
150   of the men who have great power and honor in this place;

these are leaders of the people who defend the towers
of the city by their counsels and straight judgments.
They are Triptolemos, shrewd in counsel, and Dioklos,
Polyxeinos and Eumolpos, untainted by blame,
155   Dolichos and our manly father,
and everyone has a wife managing his mansion.
No woman there, when she first looks upon you,
will dishonor your appearance and remove you from the mansion,
but each will receive you, for indeed you look like a goddess.
160   If you wish, wait here for us to go to the mansion
of our father and tell our deep-girded mother, Metaneira,
all these things from beginning to end, hoping that
she will bid you come to our mansion and not search for another's.
A growing son is being reared in the well-built mansion,
165   born late in her life, much wished for and welcome.
If you should bring him up to reach puberty,
some tender woman seeing you could easily
be envious; such rewards for rearing him she'll give you."
So she spoke, and the goddess nodded her head in assent,
170   and they proudly carried their shining vessels filled with water.
Swiftly they reached their father's great mansion and quickly told
their mother what they had seen and heard. And she commanded them
to go forthwith and invite her to come for copious wages.
And they, as deer or heifers in the season of spring,
175   sated in their hearts with pasture frisk over a meadow,
held up the folds of their lovely robes
and darted along the hollow wagon-road, as their flowing hair
tossed about their shoulders, like the flowers of the crocus.
They met the glorious goddess near the road where
180   they had left her before; and then they led her to their father's
house. And the goddess walked behind them, brooding
in her dear heart, with her head covered, while a dark
cloak swirled about her tender feet.
Soon they reached the house of Zeus-cherished Keleos
185   and through the portico they went where their lady mother
sat by a pillar, which supported the close-fitted roof,

holding a child, a young blossom, on her lap; they ran
near her, and the goddess stepped on the threshold and touched
the roof with her head and filled the doorway with divine radiance.
190 Awe, reverence and pale fear seized the mother;
and she yielded her seat to the goddess and asked her to sit.
But Demeter, the bringer of seasons and splendid gifts,
did not want to sit on the lustrous seat;
she kept silent and cast down her beautiful eyes
195 until Iambe, knowing her duties, placed in front of her
a well-fitted seat and over it she threw a white fleece.
Demeter sat on it and with her hands she held in front of her a veil,
remaining on the seat for long, speechless and brooding,
doing nothing and speaking to nobody.
200 And without laughing or tasting food and drink
she sat pining with longing for her deep-girded daughter
until Iambe, knowing her duties, with her jokes
and many jests induced the pure and mighty one
to smile and laugh and have a gracious temper.
205 At later times, too, Iambe was able to please her moods.
Metaneira now filled a cup with wine and gave it
to her, but she refused it; it was not right for her, she said,
to drink red wine. She asked them to give her a drink
of barley-meal and water mixed with tender pennyroyal.
210 She mixed the drink and gave it to the goddess, as she had asked,
and mighty Deo accepted it, complying with holy custom.
Then among them fair-girded Metaneira started speaking.
"I salute you, lady, because I think you were born to noble
and not to lowly parents. Modesty and grace show
215 in your eyes, as if you were the child of law-giving kings.
But man must take the gifts of gods even when they are
grieved by them, for on their necks there is a yoke.
And now since you have come here, what is mine will be yours.
Nurture this child of mine, whom unhoped for and late-born
220 the gods have granted me, in answer to my many prayers.
If you should bring him up to reach the age of puberty,
some tender woman seeing you could easily

7

be envious; such rewards for rearing him I will give you."
Fair-wreathed Demeter addressed her in turn:
225 "I salute you too, lady; may the gods grant you good
things. I will gladly accept the child as you ask me.
I will nurture him and I don't think that for his nurse's foolishness
either a spell or the Undercutter will harm him.
I know a remedy by far mightier than the tree-felling creature,
230 and for harmful bewitching I know a noble antidote."
With these words she received him to her fragrant bosom
and immortal arms, and the mother rejoiced in her heart.
Thus the fine son of prudent Keleos,
Demophoön, to whom fair-girded Metaneira gave birth,
235 was nurtured by her in the palace; and he grew up like a god,
not eating food or nursing at his mother's breast.
As if he were the child of a god, Demeter anointed him with ambrosia,
holding him to her bosom and breathing on him sweetly.
At night she hid him like a firebrand in the blazing fire,
240 secretly from his dear parents. To them it was a miracle
how he blossomed forth and looked like the gods.
And she would have made him ageless and immortal,
if fair-girded Metaneira, thinking foolish thoughts
and keeping watch by night from her fragrant chamber,
245 had not seen her; she raised a cry, striking her thighs
in fear for her child, and blindness entered her mind,
and weeping she spoke winged words:
"Demophoön, my child, this stranger hides you
in a great fire, bringing me grief and painful care."
250 Thus she spoke wailing, and the splendid goddess heard her.
The shafts of terrible anger shot through Demeter,
the fair-wreathed, who then with her immortal hands
took from the blazing fire and placed on the ground
the dear child born in the queen's mansion,
255 and at the same time addressed fair-girded Metaneira:
"Men are too foolish to know ahead of time
the measure of good and evil which is yet to come.
You too were greatly blinded by your foolishness.

The relentless water of the Styx by which gods swear
260   be my witness: immortal and ageless forever
would I have made your dear son and granted him everlasting honor;
but now it is not possible for him to escape the fate of death.
Yet honor everlasting shall be his because
he climbed on my knees and slept in my arms.
265   But in due time and as the years revolve for him,
the sons of the Eleusinians will join in war
and dreadful battle against each other forever.
I am Demeter the honored, the greatest
benefit and joy to undying gods and to mortals.
270   But come now, let all the people build me
a great temple and beneath it an altar under the steep walls
of the city, above Kallichoron, on the rising hill.
I myself shall introduce rites so that later
you may propitiate my mind by their right performance."
275   With these words the goddess changed her size and form
and sloughed off old age, as beauty was wafted about her.
From her fragrant veils a lovely smell
emanated, and from the immortal skin of the goddess a light
shone afar, as her blond hair streamed down over her shoulders,
280   and the sturdy mansion was filled with radiance as if from lightning.
Out she went through the mansion. The queen staggered,
and she remained speechless for a long time, forgetting
to pick her growing child up from the floor.
His sisters heard his pitiful voice,
285   and they ran from their well-spread beds; and then one
took up the child in her arms and held him to her bosom.
Another revived the fire and yet a third rushed
with her tender feet to rouse her mother from her fragrant chamber.
They gathered round the squirming child, bathed him
290   and fondled him, but his heart was not soothed,
for surely lesser nurses and governesses held him now.
All night long they propitiated the glorious goddess,
quaking with fear, and as soon as dawn appeared
they told the truth to Keleos, whose power reached far,

9

295 as the fair-wreathed goddess Demeter had ordered them.
He then called to assembly the people of every district
and bade them build an opulent temple to lovely-haired Demeter
and make an altar on the rising hill.
And they listened to his speech, and obeying forthwith
300 they built it as he ordered; and the temple took shape according to divine decree.
Now when they finished the temple and refrained from labor,
each man went to his home, but blond Demeter,
sitting there apart from all the blessed ones,
kept on wasting with longing for her deep-girded daughter.
305 Onto the much-nourishing earth she brought a year
most dreadful and harsh for men; no seed
in the earth sprouted, for fair-wreathed Demeter concealed it.
In vain the oxen drew many curved plows over the fields,
and in vain did much white barley fall into the ground.
310 And she would have destroyed the whole race of mortal men
with painful famine and would have deprived
the Olympians of the glorious honor of gifts and sacrifices,
if Zeus had not perceived this and pondered in his mind.
First he sent golden-winged Iris to invite
315 the lovely-haired Demeter of the fair form.
He spoke to her and she obeyed Zeus, the son of Kronos and lord
of dark clouds, and ran swiftly mid-way between earth and heaven.
She reached the town of Eleusis rich in sacrifices,
found the dark-veiled Demeter in the temple
320 and spoke, uttering winged words to her:
"Demeter, Zeus the father, whose wisdom never wanes,
invites you to come among the tribes of the immortal gods.
But come and let not the word of Zeus be unaccomplished."
Thus she spoke begging her, but her mind was not persuaded.
325 So then again the father sent forth all the blessed
immortal gods. They ran to her, and each in his turn
summoned her and gave her many beautiful gifts
and whatever honors she might want to choose among the immortals.
But no one could persuade the mind and thought
330 of the angry goddess who stubbornly spurned their offers.

She said she would never set foot on fragrant Olympos
and never allow the grain in the earth to sprout forth
before seeing with her eyes her fair-faced daughter.
So when loud-thundering, far-seeing Zeus heard this,
335   he sent Argeiphontes of the golden wand to Erebos.
His mission was to win Hades over with gentle words,
and bring Persephone out of misty darkness
to light and among the gods, so that her mother
might see her with her eyes and desist from anger.
340   Hermes did not disobey and, leaving his Olympian seat,
with eager speed plunged into the depths of the earth.
He found the lord inside his dwelling,
sitting on his bed with his revered spouse; she was
in many ways reluctant and missed her mother, who far
345   from the works of the blessed gods was devising a plan.
Mighty Argeiphontes stood near and addressed him:
"Hades, dark-haired lord of those who have perished,
Zeus the father bids you bring noble Persephone
out of Erebos and among the gods, so that her mother,
350   seeing her with her eyes, may desist from anger
and dreadful wrath against the gods; because she is contemplating
a great scheme to destroy the feeble races of earth-born men,
hiding the seed under the earth and abolishing the honors
of the immortals. Her anger is dreadful, and she does not mingle
355   with the gods, but apart from them in a fragrant temple
she sits, dwelling in the rocky town of Eleusis."
Thus he spoke and Aidoneus, lord of the nether world,
with smiling brows obeyed the behests of Zeus the king
and speedily gave his command to prudent-minded Persephone:
360   "Persephone, go to your dark-robed mother,
with a gentle spirit and temper in your breast,
and in no way be more dispirited than the other gods.
I shall not be an unfitting husband among the immortals,
as I am father Zeus' own brother. When you are here
365   you shall be mistress of everything which lives and moves;
your honors among the immortals shall be the greatest,

and those who wrong you shall always be punished,
if they do not propitiate your spirit with sacrifices,
performing sacred rites and making due offerings."
370 Thus he spoke and wise Persephone rejoiced
and swiftly sprang up for joy, but he himself *virginity*
gave her to eat a honey-sweet pomegranate seed,
contriving secretly about her, so that she might not spend
all her days again with dark-robed, revered Demeter.
375 Aidoneus, Ruler of Many, harnessed nearby
the immortal horses up to the golden chariot.
She mounted the chariot, and next to her mighty Argeiphontes
took the reins and the whip in his own hands
and sped out of the halls, as the horses flew readily.
380 Soon they reached the end of the long path, and neither
the sea nor the water of rivers nor the grassy glens
and mountain-peaks checked the onrush of the immortal horses,
but they went over all these, traversing the lofty air.
He drove them and then halted near the fragrant temple
385 where fair-wreathed Demeter stayed. When she saw them,
she rushed as a maenad does, along a shady woodland on the mountains.
Persephone on her part, when she saw the beautiful eyes
of her mother, leaving chariot and horses, leaped down
to run and, throwing her arms around her mother's neck, embraced her.
390 And as Demeter still held her dear child in her arms,
her mind suspected trickery, and in awful fear she withdrew
from fondling her and forthwith asked her a question:
"Child, when you were below, did you perchance partake
of food? Speak out, that we both may know.
395 If your answer is no, coming up from loathsome Hades,
you shall dwell both with me and with father Kronion,
lord of dark clouds, honored by all the immortals.
Otherwise, you shall fly and go to the depths of the earth
to dwell there a third of the seasons in the year,
400 spending two seasons with me and the other immortals.
Whenever the earth blooms with every kind of sweet-smelling
springflower, you shall come up again from misty darkness,

a great wonder for gods and mortal men.
With what trick did the mighty All-receiver deceive you?"
405 Facing her now, beautiful Persephone replied:
"Surely, Mother, I shall tell you the whole truth.
When Hermes, the helpful swift messenger, came
from father Zeus and the other heavenly dwellers
to fetch me from Erebos, so that seeing me with your eyes
410 you might desist from your anger and dreadful wrath against the immortals,
I myself sprang up for joy, but Aidoneus slyly placed
in my hands a pomegranate seed, sweet as honey to eat.
Against my will and by force he made me taste of it.
How he abducted me through the shrewd scheming of Kronides,
415 my father, and rode away carrying me to the depths of the earth
I shall explain and rehearse every point as you are asking.
All of us maidens in a delightful meadow,
Leukippe, Phaino, Electra, Ianthe,
Melite, Iache, Rhodeia, Kallirhoe,
420 Melobosis, Tyche, Okyrhoe with a face like a flower,
Chryseis, Ianeira, Akaste, Admete,
Rhodope, Plouto, lovely Kalypso,
Styx, Ourania, charming Galaxaura,   *known for being strong,*
battle-stirring Pallas, and arrow-pouring Artemis,   *determined for preserving*
425 were playing and picking lovely flowers with our hands,   *virginity.*
mingling soft crocuses and irises with hyacinths
and the flowers of the rose and lilies, a wonder to the eye,
and the narcissus which the wide earth grows crocus-colored.
So I myself was picking them with joy, but the earth beneath
430 gave way and from it the mighty lord and All-receiver
leaped out. He carried me under the earth in his golden chariot,
though I resisted and shouted with shrill voice.
I am telling you the whole truth, even though it grieves me."
So then all day long, being one in spirit,
435 they warmed each other's hearts and minds in many ways
with loving embraces, and an end to sorrow came for their hearts,
as they took joys from each other and gave in return.
Hekate of the shining headband came near them

13

and many times lovingly touched the daughter of pure Demeter.
440   From then on this lady became her attendant and follower.
Far-seeing, loud-thundering Zeus sent them a messenger,
lovely-haired Rhea, to bring her dark-veiled mother
among the races of the gods, promising to give her
whatever honors she might choose among the immortal gods.
445   With a nod of his head he promised that, as the year revolved,
her daughter could spend one portion of it in the misty darkness
and the other two with her mother and the other immortals.
He spoke and the goddess did not disobey the behests of Zeus.
Speedily she rushed down from the peaks of Olympos
450   and came to Rharion, life-giving udder of the earth
in the past, and then no longer life-giving but lying idle
without a leaf. It was now hiding the white barley
according to the plan of fair-ankled Demeter, but later
the fields would be plumed with long ears of grain,
455   as the spring waxed, and the rich furrows on the ground
would teem with ears to be bound into sheaves by withies.
There she first landed from the unharvested ether.
Joyfully they beheld each other and rejoiced in their hearts;
and Rhea of the shining headband addressed her thus:
460   "Come, child! Far-seeing, loud-thundering Zeus invites you
to come among the races of the gods and promises to give you
whatever honors you wish among the immortal gods.
With a nod of his head he promised you that, as the year revolves,
your daughter could spend one portion of it in the misty darkness
465   and the other two with you and the other immortals.
With a nod of his head he said it would thus be brought to pass.
But obey me, my child! Come and do not nurse
unrelenting anger against Kronion, lord of dark clouds;
Soon make the life-giving seed grow for men."
470   Thus she spoke and fair-wreathed Demeter did not disobey,
but swiftly made the seed sprout out of the fertile fields.
The whole broad earth teemed with leaves and flowers;
and she went to the kings who administer the laws,
Triptolemos and Diokles, smiter of horses, and mighty Eumolpos

475 and Keleos, leader of the people, and showed them the
celebration of holy rites, and explained to all,
to Triptolemos, to Polyxeinos and also to Diokles,
the awful mysteries not to be transgressed, violated
or divulged, because the tongue is restrained by reverence for the gods.
480 Whoever on this earth has seen these is blessed,
but he who has no part in the holy rites has
another lot as he wastes away in dank darkness.
After the splendid Demeter had counseled the kings in everything,
she and her daughter went to Olympos for the company of the other gods.
485 There they dwell beside Zeus who delights in thunder,
commanding awe and reverence; thrice blessed is he
of men on this earth whom they gladly love.
Soon to his great house they send as guest
Ploutos, who brings wealth to mortal men.
490 But come now, you who dwell in the fragrant town of Eleusis,
sea-girt Paros and rocky Antron,
mighty mistress Deo, bringer of seasons and splendid gifts,
both you and your daughter, beauteous Persephone,
for my song kindly grant me possessions pleasing the heart,
495 and I shall remember you and another song, too.

3. TO APOLLON

1 I shall remember not to neglect Apollon who shoots afar.
The gods of the house of Zeus tremble at his coming,
and indeed all spring up from their seats
as he approaches, stringing his splendid bow.
5 Leto alone remains by Zeus who delights in thunder
and she is the one to unstring Apollon's bow and close the quiver;
from his mighty shoulders with her hands she takes
the bow and hangs it up on a golden peg
on her father's pillar, and after that she leads him to a seat.

15

10   Then his father offers him nectar in a golden goblet
     and drinks a toast to his dear son; and then
     the other gods sit down as mighty Leto rejoices,
     because she bore a valiant son who carries the bow.
     Hail, O blessed Leto, because you bore illustrious children,
15   lord Apollon and arrow-pouring Artemis,
     her on Ortygia and him on rocky Delos,
     as you leaned against the towering mass of the Kynthian hill,
     very near a palm tree by the streams of the Inopos.
     How shall I match the hymns already sung in your honor?
20   For everywhere, Phoibos, the field of singing is your domain,
     both on the islands and the mainland which nurtures heifers.
     All peaks and high ridges of lofty mountains
     and rivers flowing seawards and harbors of the sea
     and beaches sloping toward it give you pleasure.
25   Shall I sing how first Leto bore you, a joy to mortals,
     as she leaned against Mount Kynthos, on the rocky and sea-girt
     island of Delos, while on either side a dark wave
     swept landwards impelled by shrill winds?
     Thence you arose to rule over all mortal men:
30   over the inhabitants of Crete and of the town of Athens,
     of Aigina and Euboea, famous for ships,
     of Aigai and Eiresiai and Peparethos by the sea,
     of Thracian Athos and Pelion's lofty peaks,
     of Thracian Samos and Ida's shady mountains,
35   of Skyros and Phokaia and Autokane's steep heights,
     of well-built Imbros and Lemnos, enveloped in haze,
     of holy Lesbos, realm of Makar, son of Aiolos,
     of Chios, brightest of all the islands lying in the sea,
     of craggy Mimas and the lofty peaks of Korykos,
40   of shimmering Klaros and Aisagee's steep heights,
     of well-watered Samos and Mykale's towering peaks,
     of Miletos and Kos, city of Meropian men,
     of rugged Knidos and wind-swept Karpathos,
     of Naxos and Paros and rocky Rhenaia.
45   So many places did Leto visit, in travail with the far-shooter,
     searching for a land which would give him a home.

But they trembled greatly in fear, and none dared—
not even the richer ones—to be a host to Phoibos,
until indeed mighty Leto set foot on Delos
50 and made an inquiry, addressing winged words to her:
"Delos, would you want to be the abode of my son,
Phoibos Apollon, and to house him in an opulent temple?
For it cannot escape you that no other will touch you
since I think you shall never be rich in oxen or sheep
55 and shall never produce vintage nor grow an abundance of plants.
If you have a temple for Apollon who shoots from afar,
then all men shall gather here and bring
hecatombs, and the ineffably rich savor of burning fat
shall always rise, and you shall feed your dwellers
60 from the hands of strangers, since your soil is barren."
So she spoke. Then Delos rejoiced and gave this answer:
"Leto, most glorious daughter of great Koios,
I would gladly receive your offspring, the lord
who shoots from afar; since truly the sound of my name
65 is no pleasure to men, thereby I would be greatly honored.
But, Leto, I shall not hide the fear this word brings me.
They say that Apollon will be haughty
and greatly lord it over the immortal gods
and the mortal men of the barley-bearing earth.
70 Thus I dreadfully fear in my heart and soul
lest, when he first sees the light of the sun,
scorning an island whose ground is rocky,
he overturn me with his feet and push me into the deep sea.
And there a great billow will incessantly flood me
75 up to my highest peak, while he arrives at another land,
where it may please him to establish a temple and wooded groves.
Then polyps will settle on me and black seals on me
will make their carefree abodes where there are no people.
But, goddess, if only you would deign to swear a great oath,
80 that here first he would build a beautiful temple
to be an oracle for men and afterwards
. . . .
among all men, since today many are his names."

17

So she spoke, and Leto swore the god's great oath:
"Earth be my witness and the wide heaven above

85   and the cascading water of the Styx, which is the greatest
and most awful oath among the blessed gods,
that here there shall always be a fragrant altar and temple
for Phoibos and that he shall honor you above all others."
And when she swore and completed her oath

90   the far-shooting lord's expected birth brought great joy to Delos;
and for nine days and nine nights Leto was racked
by travail unexpected. The goddesses were all with her—
the best ones, that is—such as Dione, Rhea,
Ichnaian Themis, loud-groaning Amphitrite

95   and other immortal goddesses save white-armed Hera,
who sat in the palace of cloud-gathering Zeus.
Only Eileithyia, goddess of labor pains, did not find out,
for she sat on top of Olympos under golden clouds,
through the counsels of white-armed Hera, who restrained her

100   out of jealousy, because fair-tressed Leto
was about to give birth to a mighty and blameless son.
They sent Iris forth from the well-built island
to bring Eileithyia, promising a great necklace
nine cubits long and held together by golden threads.

105   And they bid Iris call her apart from white-armed Hera
lest, with her words, she turn Eileithyia back from going.
When swift Iris, fleet of foot as the wind, heard this,
she set out to run and quickly traversed all the midspace,
and when she reached lofty Olympos, the seat of the gods,

110   forthwith she called Eileithyia out of the palace
to the doors and, addressing her with winged words,
told her all, as she had been commanded by the Olympian goddesses.
She did persuade her heart in her dear breast
and as they went their gait was like that of timid doves.

115   And when Eileithyia, goddess of travail, set foot on Delos,
the pains of labor seized Leto, and she yearned to give birth.
She threw her two arms round the palm tree, and propped her knees
on the soft meadow while the earth beneath her was all smiles.

Apollon sprang forth to the light, and all the goddesses screamed.
120 Then, noble Phoibos, the goddesses bathed you pure and clean
with fresh water and swaddled you in a white sheet,
fine and new-woven, and around you they wrapped a golden band.
Nor indeed did his mother nurse Apollon of the golden sword
but Themis poured for him nectar and lovely ambrosia
125 with her immortal hands, and Leto rejoiced
for giving birth to a mighty son who carries the bow.
But when, O Phoibos, you devoured this food for immortals,
neither golden bands could hold you as you struggled
nor bonds restrain you, for their ends came loose.
130 Forthwith among the goddesses spoke Phoibos Apollon:
"My wish is to hold dear the lyre and the curved bow
and to prophesy for men the unerring will of Zeus."
With these words the long-haired, far-shooting god
walked away over the earth and its wide roads, and all
135 the goddesses were dazzled while all Delos with gold
[was laden, looking upon the offspring of Zeus and Leto,
for joy, because from among the islands and the mainland
a god chose her for his dwelling and loved her dearly in his heart]
bloomed as does a mountain peak with the flowers of the forest.
140 You yourself, far-shooting lord of the silver bow,
sometimes set foot on rocky Kynthos
while at other times you roam among islands and men.
Many temples and wooded groves are yours,
and all the peaks and towering crags of lofty mountains
145 and rivers flowing forth to the sea are dear to you.
But it is in Delos, O Phoibos, that your heart delights the most,
for Ionians with trailing garments gather there
in your honor together with their children and modest wives.
And with boxing matches, dancing and song,
150 they delight you and remember you whenever they hold the contests.
Whoever comes upon the Ionians, when they are gathered,
might think they were forever immortal and ageless.
For he would see their grace and delight his soul,
looking upon the fair-girded women and the men

155   with their swift ships and their many possessions.
There is also a great wonder of everlasting renown,
the Delian maidens, followers of the lord who shoots from afar.
After they first praise Apollon with a hymn
and now again Leto and arrow-pouring Artemis,
160   they tell of men and women who lived long ago
and sing a hymn, charming the races of men.
The tongues of all men and their noisy chatter
they know how to mimic; such is their skill in composing the song
that each man might think he himself were speaking.
165   But now may Apollon and Artemis be propitious;
and all you maidens farewell. I ask you to call me to mind
in time to come whenever some man on this earth,
a stranger whose suffering never ends, comes here and asks:
"Maidens, which of the singers, a man wont to come here,
170   is to you the sweetest, and in whom do you most delight?"
Do tell him in unison that I am he,
a blind man, dwelling on the rocky island of Chios,
whose songs shall all be the best in time to come.
And I will carry your renown as far as I roam
175   over the lands of men and their cities of fair locations.
Indeed they will not doubt this because it is true.
And I shall not cease to hymn far-shooting Apollon,
lord of the silver bow and child of lovely-haired Leto.
O Lord, yours is Lykia and Meonia the lovely
180   and Miletos, too, the enchanting city by the sea,
and you again greatly rule over wave-washed Delos.
The son of glorious Leto goes to rocky Pytho,
playing his hollow lyre,
and wearing garments divine and fragrant; his lyre
185   struck by the golden plectrum gives an enchanting sound.
Thence, fleet as thought, he leaves the earth for Olympos
and goes to the palace of Zeus and the company of the other gods.
Forthwith the immortals take interest in his song and lyre,
and all the Muses, answering with beautiful voices,
190   hymn the divine gifts of the gods and the hardships

brought upon men by the immortal gods.
Men live an unresourceful and thoughtless life, unable
to find a cure for death and a charm to repel old age.
And the fair-tressed Graces and the kindly Seasons
195   and Harmonia and Hebe and Aphrodite, the daughter of Zeus,
dance, each holding the other's wrist.
Among them sings one, neither ugly nor slight of stature
but truly of great size and marvelous aspect,
arrow-pouring Artemis, Apollon's twin sister.
200   And with them play Ares and keen-eyed Argeiphontes;
Phoibos Apollon, his step high and stately,
plays the lyre, enveloped in the brilliance
from his glittering feet and well-woven garment.
And Leto of the golden tresses and Zeus the counselor
205   rejoice in their great souls as they look upon
their dear son playing among the immortals.
How shall I match the hymns already sung in your honor?
Or am I to sing of you as wooer and lover of maidens,
sing how, wooing the daughter of Azas, you raced
210   against godlike Ischys Elationides, possessed of good horses,
or against Phorbas sprung from Triops or against Ereutheus?
Or in the company of Leukippos' wife,
you on foot and he with his horses? He surely was as good as Triops!
Or am I to sing how at first you went all over the earth,
215   seeking the seat of an oracle, O far-shooting Apollon?
To Pieria you first descended from Olympos
and made your way past sandy Lektos and the Ainianes
and Perrhaiboi; and soon you reached Iolkos
and set foot on Kenaion in Euboea, renowned for ships;
220   you stood on the Lelantine plain, but it did not please
your heart to build a temple with wooded groves.
From there, O far-shooting Apollon, you crossed Euripos
and went along a sacred green mountain, and leaving
you came to Mykalessos and grassy-bedded Teumessos.
225   Then you arrived at the forest-covered abode of Thebe;
no mortal as yet lived in sacred Thebe,

21

and at that time there were no paths or roads yet
throughout the wheat-bearing plain of Thebe, but forests covered it.
Thence, O splendid Apollon, you went onward
230   to reach Onchestos, the fair grove of Poseidon,
where a new-broken colt, vexed as he is at drawing
the beautiful chariot, slows down to breathe, as its noble driver
leaps down from the chariot and goes his way; and the horses
for some time rattle the empty chariot, free from their master's control.
235   And if they should break the chariot in the wooded grove,
the horses are taken away but the tilted chariot is left behind.
For such is the ancient custom: they pray to the lord
while to the god's lot falls the custody of the chariot.
You soon left that place, O far-shooting Apollon,
240   and then reached the beautiful streams of Kephissos
which pours forth its fair-flowing water from Lilaia.
And, O worker from afar, you crossed it and many-towered Okalea,
and thence you arrived at grassy Haliartos.
You set foot on Telphousa, where the peaceful place
245   pleased you, and so you built a temple with wooded groves.
Standing very close to her you spoke these words:
"Telphousa, here I intend to build a beautiful temple
to be an oracle for men who will always
bring to me here unblemished hecatombs;
250   and as many as dwell on fertile Peloponnesos
and on Europe and throughout the sea-girt islands
will consult it. It is my wish to give them unerring
advice, making prophecies inside the opulent temple."
With these words Phoibos Apollon laid out the foundations,
255   broad and very long from beginning to end; Telphousa saw this
and with anger in her heart she spoke these words:
"Lord Phoibos, worker from afar, I shall put a word in your heart,
since you intend to build a beautiful temple in this place,
to be an oracle for men who will always
260   bring there unblemished hecatombs.
Yet I will speak out, and you mark my word in your heart.
The pounding of swift horses and mules

watering at my sacred springs will always annoy you,
and men will prefer to gaze upon
265 the well-made chariots and the pounding, swift-footed horses
than upon the great temple and the many possessions therein.
But please listen to me—you are a lord better and mightier
than I, and your power is very great—
build at Krisa beneath the fold of Parnassos.
270 There neither beautiful chariots will rattle nor swift-footed
horses will pound about the well-built altar.
But to you as Iepaieon the glorious races of men
will bring gifts, and with delighted heart you will receive
beautiful sacrificial offerings from those dwelling about."
275 With these words Telphousa swayed his mind, so that hers alone,
and not the Far-shooter's should be the glory of the land.
You soon left that place, O far-shooting Apollon,
and reached the city of the Phlegyes, those insolent men,
who dwelt on this earth, with no regard for Zeus,
280 in a beautiful glen near the lake Kephisis.
From there you went rushing to a mountain ridge,
and you reached Krisa beneath snowy Parnassos,
a foothill looking westwards, with a rock
hanging above it and a hollow and rough glen
285 running below it. There the lord Phoibos Apollon
resolved to make a lovely temple and spoke these words:
"Here I intend to build a beautiful temple
to be an oracle for men who shall always
bring to this place unblemished hecatombs;
290 and as many as dwell on fertile Peloponnesos
and on Europe and throughout the sea-girt islands
will consult it. It is my wish to give them unerring
advice, making prophecies inside the opulent temple."
With these words Phoibos Apollon laid out the foundations,
295 broad and very long from beginning to end; and on them
the sons of Erginos, Trophonios and Agamedes,
dear to the immortal gods, placed a threshold of stone.
And the numberless races of men built the temple all around

with hewn stones, to be a theme of song forever.
300   Near it there was a fair-flowing spring, where the lord,
son of Zeus, with his mighty bow, killed a she-dragon,
a great, glutted and fierce monster, which inflicted
many evils on the men of the land—many on them
and many on their slender-shanked sheep; for she was bloodthirsty.
305   And once from golden-throned Hera she received and reared
dreadful and baneful Typhaon, a scourge to mortals.
Hera once bore him in anger at father Zeus,
when indeed Kronides gave birth to glorious Athena
from his head; and mighty Hera was quickly angered
310   and spoke to the gathering of the immortal gods:
"All gods and all goddesses, hear from me
how cloud-gathering Zeus begins to dishonor me
first, since he made me his mindfully devoted wife,
and now apart from me gave birth to gray-eyed Athena,
315   who excels among all the blessed immortals.
But my son, Hephaistos, whom I myself bore
has grown to be weak-legged and lame among the blessed gods.
I took him with my own hands and cast him into the broad sea.
But Thetis, the silver-footed daughter of Nereus,
320   received him and with her sisters took him in her care.
I wish she had done the blessed gods some other favor!
O stubborn and wily one! What else will you now devise?
How dared you alone give birth to gray-eyed Athena?
Would not I have borne her?—I, who was called your very own
325   among the immortals who dwell in the broad sky?
[325a Take thought now, lest I devise some evil for you in return!]
And now, I shall contrive to have born to me
a child who will excel among the immortals.
And to our sacred wedlock I shall bring no shame,
nor visit your bed, but I shall pass my time
330   far from you, among the immortal gods."
With these words she went apart from the gods very angry.
Then forthwith mighty, cow-eyed Hera prayed
and with the flat of her hand struck the ground and spoke:

"Hear me now, Earth and broad Sky above,
335 and you Titans from whom gods and men are descended
and who dwell beneath the earth round great Tartaros.
Harken to me, all of you, and apart from Zeus grant me a child,
in no wise of inferior strength; nay, let him be stronger
than Zeus by as much as far-seeing Zeus is stronger than Kronos."
340 Thus she cried out and lashed the earth with her stout hand.
Then the life-giving earth was moved and Hera saw it,
and her heart was delighted at the thought of fulfillment.
From then on, and until a full year came to its end,
she never came to the bed of contriving Zeus,
345 nor pondered for him sagacious counsels,
sitting as before on her elaborate chair,
but staying in temples, where many pray,
cow-eyed, mighty Hera delighted in her offerings.
But when the months and the days reached their destined goal,
350 and the seasons arrived as the year revolved,
she bore dreadful and baneful Typhaon, a scourge to mortals,
whose aspect resembled neither god's nor man's.
Forthwith cow-eyed, mighty Hera took him and, piling evil
upon evil, she commended him to the care of the she-dragon.
355 He worked many evils on the glorious races of men,
and she brought their day of doom to those who met her,
until the lord far-shooting Apollon shot her
with a mighty arrow; rent with insufferable pains,
she lay panting fiercely and writhing on the ground.
360 The din was ineffably awesome, and throughout the forest
she was rapidly thrusting her coils hither and thither; with a gasp
she breathed out her gory soul, while Phoibos Apollon boasted:
"Rot now right here on the man-nourishing earth;
you shall not ever again be an evil bane for living men
365 who eat the fruit of the earth that nurtures many
and will bring to this place unblemished hecatombs,
not shall Typhoeus or ill-famed Chimaira
ward off woeful death for you, but right here
the black earth and the flaming sun will make you rot."

25

370   Thus he spoke boasting, and darkness covered her eyes.
And the holy fury of Helios made her rot away;
hence the place is now called Pytho, and people
call the lord by the name of Pytheios, because on that spot
the fury of piercing Helios made the monster rot away.

375   At last Phoibos Apollon knew in his mind
why the fair-flowing spring had deceived him.
So in anger against Telphousa he set out and quickly reached her
and, standing very close to her, uttered these words:
"Telphousa, you were not destined, after all, to deceive my mind

380   by keeping this lovely place to pour forth your fair-flowing water.
The glory of this place will be mine, too, not yours alone."
Thus spoke the lord, far-shooting Apollon, and pushed down on her a cliff,
and with a shower of rocks he covered her streams;
then he built himself an altar in the wooded grove,

385   very close to the fair-flowing stream, and there all men
pray calling upon him as the Telphousian lord,
because he shamed the streams of sacred Telphousa.
And then indeed Phoibos Apollon pondered in his mind
what kind of men he should bring in to celebrate his rites

390   and be his ministers in rocky Pytho.
As he pondered these thoughts, he descried a swift ship
on the wine-dark sea; there were many noble men on it,
Cretans from Minoan Knossos, who for the lord
make sacrificial offerings and proclaim the decrees

395   of Phoibos Apollon of the golden sword, whatever he may say
when he prophesies from the laurel below the dells of Parnassos.
To sandy Pylos and its native dwellers
they sailed in a black ship for barter and goods,
and Phoibos Apollon went to meet them at sea

400   and, looking like a dolphin in shape, he leaped on
the swift ship and lay on it like some great and awesome monster.
And it entered no man's mind to know who he was
as he lunged about and shook the timbers of the ship.
They sat on the ship, afraid and dumbfounded,

405   and neither slacked the sheets throughout the hollow black ship

nor lowered the sail of the dark-prowed keel.
But as they had fixed its direction with oxhide lines,
so they sailed on; for a rushing south wind pressed
the swift ship on from behind. First sailing past Maleia
410 and then past the land of Lakonia, they reached
a sea-crowned city, a place of Helios who gladdens mortals,
Tainaron, where always graze the long-fleeced sheep
of lord Helios and are the tenants of the delightful place.
They wanted to put the ship to shore there and land
415 to contemplate the great portent and see with their eyes
whether the monster would remain on the deck of the hollow ship
or leap into the briny swell which teems with fishes.
But the well-wrought ship did not obey the helm,
and off the shore of fertile Peloponnesos
420 went her way as the lord, far-shooting Apollon, easily
steered her course with a breeze. She traversed her path
and reached Arene and lovely Argyphea,
and Thryon, the ford of Alpheios, and well-built Aipy,
and sandy Pylos and its native dwellers.
425 She sailed past Krounoi and Chalkis and Dymê
and splendid Elis, where the Epeioi are lords.
When she was headed for Pherai, exulting in the tail wind
sent by Zeus, from under the clouds the lofty mountain of Ithake
appeared, and Doulichion and Samê and wooded Zakynthos.
430 But when the shore of Peloponnesos was behind her,
and there loomed in the distance Krisa's boundless gulf,
which cuts off from the mainland the fertile Peloponnesos,
there came, decreed by Zeus, a great and fair west wind
rushing down vehemently from the clear sky, so that the ship
435 might soon traverse in speed the briny water of the sea.
Then they sailed back toward the dawn and the sun,
and the lord Apollon, son of Zeus, was their leader
until they reached the harbor of conspicuous Krisa,
rich in vineyards, where the seafaring ship grounded on the sands.
440 And there the lord, far-shooting Apollon, leaped from the ship,
like a star at midday, as flashes of light

flew about and their brilliance touched the sky.
Through the precious tripods his sanctuary he entered,
to light a flame with his gleaming shafts,
445 enveloping all of Krisa in light; and the wives
and fair-girded daughters of the Krisians raised a cry
at the radiance of Phoibos, for he instilled in them great fear.
From there, swift as thought, he took a flying leap
back into the ship, in the form of a strong and vigorous
450 man in his prime, his mane covering his broad shoulders.
And with loud voice he uttered winged words:
"Who are you strangers and whence do you sail the watery paths?
Is it perchance for barter, or do you wander idly
over the sea like roaming pirates
455 who risk their lives to bring evil upon men of other lands?
Why do you sit thus in fear, neither going out
to shore nor stowing the tackle of your black ship?
Such indeed is the custom of men who work for their bread,
whenever on their black ship they come to land
460 from the sea, worn-out with toil, and straightway
a longing for sweet food grips their hearts."
Thus he spoke and put courage in their breasts,
and the leader of the Cretans spoke to him in answer:
"Stranger, since in no wise do you resemble a mortal
465 in build or stature, but rather look like the deathless gods,
a hearty hail to you, and may the gods grant you good fortune.
Now speak the truth to me that I may know well.
What folk is this, what land, what mortals live here?
With other designs in mind we sailed over the vast sea
470 to Pylos from Crete, whence we boast our race to hail.
Now against our will we have sailed here in our ship,
on another course and another path, and long to go home;
but some immortal has brought us here against our will."
And far-shooting Apollon addressed them and answered:
475 "Strangers, up to now you dwelt about Knossos
with its many trees; now you shall no longer be
on the homeward journey, bound for your lovely city,

your beautiful homes and dear wives, but you shall keep
my opulent temple which is honored by many men.

480 I am the son of Zeus and proudly declare I am Apollon.
I brought you here over the vast and deep sea,
entertaining no evil thoughts, but here you shall have
my opulent temple, which is greatly honored by all men,
and you shall know the will of the immortals, by whose wish

485 you shall be honored forever to the end of your days.
But come and obey at once whatever I say:
First slack the oxhide lines and lower the sails,
and then draw the swift ship onto the land,
and out of the well-trimmed keel take tackle and possessions,

490 and make an altar upon the beach of the sea;
then light a fire on it and offer white barley,
and, standing round the altar, say your prayers.
Since I, at first on the misty sea
in the form of a dolphin, leaped onto the swift ship,

495 so pray to me as Delphinios; the altar too,
shall be called Delphinian and be forever conspicuous.
After that have your meal by the swift black ship,
and pour libations to the blessed gods who dwell on Olympos.
But when you have rid yourselves of desire for sweet food,

500 come with me, singing the hymn Iepaieon,
until you reach the place where you shall keep my opulent temple."
So he spoke, and they readily heard him and obeyed.
First they lowered the sails and slacked the oxhide lines,
and by the forestays brought the mast down to the mast-holder.

505 Then they themselves landed on the beach
and drew the swift ship from the sea onto the land,
and high onto the sand, and spread long props underneath.
There, on the beach of the sea they made an altar,
then lighted a fire on it, and with offerings of white barley

510 they prayed, as he ordered, standing round the altar.
They then had their meal by the swift black ship
and poured libations to the blessed gods who dwell on Olympos.
And when they rid themselves of desire for food and drink,

they set out to go, and the lord Apollon, son of Zeus, led the way,
515 his step high and stately, and with the lyre in his hands
played a lovely tune. The Cretans followed him
to Pytho, beating time and singing the Iepaieon
in the fashion of Cretans singing a paean when the divine
Muse has put mellifluous song in their hearts.
520 They walked up the hill unwearied and soon reached
Parnassos and the lovely place where he was destined
to dwell honored by many men; he led them there
and showed them the sacred sanctuary and opulent temple.
But their spirit was roused in their dear hearts,
525 and the leader of the Cretans addressed him and asked:
"Lord, since far from our dear ones and our fatherland
you have brought us—for thus it pleased your heart—
how are we now to live? This we bid you tell us.
This charming place does not abound in vineyards or meadows
530 from which we may live well and be in the service of men."
And Apollon, the son of Zeus, smiled on them and answered:
"Foolish men and poor wretches you are for preferring
cares and toilsome hardships and straits for your hearts.
Put in your minds the word I will speak to set you at ease:
535 With a knife in his right hand let each one of you
slaughter sheep forever, and there will be an abundance
of them brought to me by the glorious races of men.
But guard my temple and receive the races of men
gathered here, and especially my direction

. . . .

540 Your word or deed shall be vain
and wantonly insolent, as is the custom of mortal men;
then you shall have other men to command you,
and by force be your masters forever.
I have told you everything; do keep it in your mind."
545 And so, son of Zeus and Leto, farewell,
and I shall remember you and another song, too.

4. TO HERMES

1   Of Hermes sing, O Muse, the son of Zeus and Maia,
     lord of Kyllene and Arcadia abounding with sheep,
     helpful messenger of the immortals, whom Maia bore,
     the fair-tressed and revered nymph, when she mingled in love
5   with Zeus; she shunned the company of the blessed gods
     and dwelt inside a thick-shaded cave, where Kronion,
     escaping the eyes of immortal gods and mortal men,
     mingled with the fair-tressed nymph in the darkness of night,
     while sweet sleep overcame white-armed Hera.
10   But when the mind of great Zeus accomplished its goal,
     and the tenth moon was set fast in the sky,
     a new-born saw the light, and uncanny deeds came to pass.
     Then she bore a child who was a shrewd and coaxing schemer,
     a cattle-rustling robber, and a bringer of dreams,
15   a watcher by night and a gate-keeper, soon destined
     to show forth glorious deeds among the immortal gods.
     Born at dawn, by midday he played his lyre,
     and at evening he stole the cattle of far-shooting Apollon,
     on the fourth of the month, the very day mighty Maia bore him.
20   After he sprang forth from his mother's immortal limbs,
     he did not remain for long lying in his holy cradle,
     but he leaped up and searched for the cattle of Apollon,
     stepping over the threshold of the high-roofed cave.
     There he found a tortoise and won boundless bliss,
25   for Hermes was the first to make a singer of a tortoise,
     which met him at the gates of the courtyard,
     grazing on the lush grass near the dwelling
     and dragging its straddling feet; and the helpful son of Zeus
     laughed when he saw it and straightway he said:
30   "Already an omen of great luck! I don't despise you.
     Hail, O shapely hoofer and companion of the feast!
     Your sight is welcome! Whence this lovely toy,
     the gleaming shell that clothes you, a tortoise living on the mountains?
     But I shall take you and bring you inside; you'll profit me.

35 And I shall not dishonor you for you will serve me first.
    Better to be inside; being at the gates is harmful for you.
    Indeed alive you shall be a charm against baneful
    witchcraft; and if you die, your singing could be beautiful."
    Thus he spoke and with both hands he raised it up
40 and ran back into his abode, carrying the lovely toy.
    There he tossed it upside down and with a chisel of gray iron
    he scooped out the life of the mountain-turtle.
    As when swift thought pierces the breast
    of a man in whom thick-coming cares churn,
45 or as when flashing glances dart from quick-rolling eyes,
    so glorious Hermes pondered word and deed at once.
    He cut measured stalks of reed and fastened them on
    by piercing through the back the shell of the tortoise;
    and skillfully he stretched oxhide round the shell
50 and on it he fixed two arms joined by a crosspiece
    from which he stretched seven harmonious strings of sheep-gut.
    And when it was finished, he held up the lovely toy
    and with the plectron struck it tunefully, and under his hand
    the lyre rang awesome. The god sang to it beautifully,
55 as on the lyre he tried improvisations, such as young men do
    at the time of feasts when they taunt and mock each other.
    He sang of Zeus Kronides and fair-sandaled Maia,
    and how they once dallied in the bond of love,
    recounting in detail his own glorious birth.
60 He also praised the handmaidens, and the splendid home of the nymph
    and the tripods throughout her dwelling, and the imperishable cauldrons.
    That is what he sang, but other matters engaged his mind.
    He carried the hollow lyre and laid it down
    in the holy cradle, and then craving for meat
65 he leaped from the fragrant dwelling and went forth scouting,
    pondering some bold wile in his mind, such as men
    who are bandits pursue when dark night falls.
    Helios was plunging down from the earth into the ocean
    with his horses and chariot, when Hermes in haste
70 reached the shaded mountains of Pieria,

where the divine cattle of the blessed gods had their stalls
and grazed on the lovely untrodden meadows.
Then the son of Maia, sharp-eyed Argeiphontes,
cut off from the herd fifty head of loud-lowing cattle.
75 Through the sandy place he drove them on a beguiling route,
turning their hoofprints round. Mindful of the artful ruse,
he reversed their hoofs, setting the front part backward
and the back part frontward and opposite to his own course.
And forthwith on the sandy beach he plaited sandals
80 of wicker-work, wondrous things of unimaginable skill,
mingling tamarisk and twigs of myrtle.
He made a bundle of fresh-grown seasonable branches
and snugly tied them as sandals under his feet,
leaves and all, just as glorious Argeiphontes
85 had plucked them from Pieria to lighten the toil of walking
by making his own device, as one does on an urgent long journey.
But an old man working on his flowering vineyard saw him,
as he pressed on toward the plain through grassy-bedded Onchestos.
The son of glorious Maia was first to address him:
90 "Old man, digging round your vines with bent shoulders,
no doubt you shall have plenty of wine when all these bear fruit.
You are to be blind to what you saw and deaf to what you heard,
and silent too when no harm is done to what is your own."
This much said, the precious cattle he drove on,
95 and glorious Hermes led them through many shaded mountains,
ravines loud-echoing with blustering winds, and flowering plains.
Most of the wondrous night, his sable accomplice, had passed,
and dawn was soon to come and send the people to work.
And the shining Selene, daughter of lord Pallas,
100 son of Megamedes, had just mounted her watch-post,
when the doughty son of Zeus drove the wide-browed
cattle of Phoibos Apollon to the river Alpheios.
Still not broken-in the cattle came to a high-roofed barn
and watering-troughs close to a remarkable meadow.
105 Then when he had grazed well the loud-lowing cattle in the pasture,
he herded them together and drove them into the barn

while they were chewing lotus and dewy galingale,
and intent on the skill of making fire he fetched much wood.
A fine branch of laurel he took and peeled with his knife

. . . .

110   tight-fitted in his palm, and up went the heated smoke.
For Hermes was the first to give us fire from fire-sticks.
He gathered many dry sticks and made a thick
and sturdy pile in a sunken pit; and the flame shone afar,
giving off a blast, as the fire burnt high.
115   While the power of glorious Hephaistos kindled the fire,
he dragged out to the door close by the fire
two curved-horned bellowing cows; for great was his strength.
They puffed as he cast them both on their backs,
and bending their necks he rolled them over and pierced their spines.
120   Task upon task he carried out and hacked the fatted meat.
He pierced with wooden spits and roasted
meat and the prized chine and dark blood,
all wrapped in guts; all this lay on the spot.
The skins he stretched on a hard and dry rock
125   and up to this day and after all these years they are there,
an endlessly long time after those events; and then
cheerful Hermes dragged the sumptuous meal
onto a smooth slab and chopped it into twelve portions
given by lot and to each he assigned perfect honor.
130   Then glorious Hermes craved for the sacred meat
because the sweet savor weakened his resolve, immortal though
he was. But not even so was his manly soul prevailed upon,
although his holy gullet greatly hankered for the meat.
But he stowed fat with much of the meat away
135   in the high-roofed barn and swiftly hung it up
as a token of his recent theft; then dry wood he gathered
and let the fire's breath consume the shaggy feet and heads.
And after the god accomplished everything in proper order,
he threw his sandals into the deep-eddying Alpheios;
140   he let the glowing embers die down and on the black ashes
strewed sand all night, as fair shone the light of Selene.

Then speedily he came back to Kyllene's shining peaks
at dawn, and no one met him on his long journey,
neither blessed god nor mortal man,
145   and no dog barked. And Hermes, the son of Zeus,
slipped through the keyhole of the dwelling sideways,
like autumnal breeze in outer form, or airy mist.
He made straight for the cave and reached its copious fane,
walking softly on his feet, not pounding as one might upon the ground.
150   Then glorious Hermes came to his cradle in haste,
and wrapped his swaddling clothes about his shoulders, like an infant
child, and lay there playing with the covers with palms
and thighs and keeping his sweet lyre on the left.
The god did not remain unnoticed by his divine mother who said:
155   "What is this, you weaver of schemes? Whence in the dead of night
are you coming, clothed in shamelessness? I surely think
that either Leto's son will shackle your arms about your ribs
and drag you through the door-way,
or you will rove the gorges as a raiding bandit.
160   Go back! Your father planted you to be a vexing care
among mortal men and deathless gods."
And Hermes spoke to her with calculated words:
"Mother, why do you fling these words at me as at an infant
child who knows but a few wicked thoughts in his mind
165   and full of fear is cowed by his mother's chiding?
But I shall be master of whatever skill is best
to provide for you and me forever; we shall not suffer,
as you bid me, to stay right here and be
the only two immortals not plied with gifts and prayers.
170   It is better to be forever in the gods' intimate circle,
rich, affluent, and with an abundance of grain, than to sit
in this dark cave; and as for honor, I, too,
shall claim the rite of which Apollon is a master.
And if my father does not allow me this, I shall surely
175   try to be, as I no doubt can, the chief of robbers.
And if the son of glorious Leto seeks to find me,
then I think he will meet with some greater loss.

For to Pytho I shall go and break my way into his great house,
whence many beautiful tripods and cauldrons
180 I shall plunder, and gold, too, and gleaming iron
and many garments; and you shall witness this if you wish."
The son of aegis-bearing Zeus and mighty Maia
with such words thus spoke to each other.
And Dawn, the early-born, was rising from deep-flowing Okeanos
185 to bring light to mortals, but Apollon
went on and reached Onchestos, the lovely and pure
grove of the loud-roaring Holder of the Earth. An old man
he found there grazing his beast, the bulwark of his vineyard,
by the road, and the son of glorious Leto addressed him first:
190 "Aged brambleberry-picker of grassy Onchestos,
I have come here from Pieria in search of my cattle,
all of them cows, and everyone with curved horns,
from my herd. The black bull was grazing alone
away from the rest and four hounds with flashing eyes,
195 like men of one mind, followed them, but the hounds and the bull
were left behind, and this is truly a great wonder.
The sun had hardly set when they strayed away
from the soft meadow and the sweet pasture.
Aged man born of old, tell me whether you have seen
200 on this road a man going after my cows."
And the old man replied to him and said:
"Friend, it is hard to tell all that one sees with his eyes;
for so many are the wayfarers traveling this road,
some of them bent on many evil things while others
205 go after what is good, and no easy task it is to know each one.
But I was digging round the hillock of my vineyard
all day long until the sun was setting;
and then, sir, I thought I saw a child—I can't be sure.
This child, an infant, too, followed the horned cows,
210 holding a staff and walking all about from side to side;
and he drove them with tails backwards and heads facing toward him."
So said the old man, and Apollon heard his words
and swiftly went his way. And then he saw a long-winged bird

and knew forthwith that the robber was the son of Zeus Kronion.
215 And Apollon, son of Zeus, speedily rushed
to holy Pylos in search of his shambling cows,
his broad shoulders enveloped in a purple cloud.
The Far-Shooter saw the tracks and said these words:
"Heavens! A truly great wonder I see with my eyes.
220 These no doubt are the tracks of straight-horned cows,
but they are turned backwards toward the flowery meadow.
These tracks belong neither to man nor to woman,
nor yet to gray wolves, nor bears, nor lions.
And I do not think they are those of a shaggy-maned centaur—
225 whoever has taken such monstrous swift strides.
Wondrous on this side of the road, they are yet more wondrous on the other."
With these words Lord Apollon, son of Zeus, rushed
and reached the mountain of Kyllene, overgrown with trees,
and the deep-shaded, rocky hiding place where the divine
230 nymph gave birth to the son of Zeus Kronion.
A delightful odor permeated the holy mountain,
and many long-shanked sheep grazed on the grass.
Then Apollon himself in haste stepped down
the stone threshold and into the gloomy cave.
235 When Zeus and Maia's son saw Apollon,
the Far-Shooter, angered about his cattle,
he snuggled into his sweet-scented swaddling-clothes;
and as ashes cover a heap of embers from tree-trunks,
so Hermes wrapped himself up when he saw the Far-Shooter.
240 Into a small space he huddled head, hands and feet,
like a freshly bathed baby courting sweet sleep,
but in truth still awake and holding the lyre under his arm.
The son of Zeus and Leto did not fail to recognize
the beautiful mountain nymph and her dear son,
245 though he was a tiny child steeped in crafty wiles.
He peered into every niche and nook of the great dwelling,
and he took a shining key and opened three vaults
filled with nectar and lovely ambrosia;
inside them lay much gold and silver

250 and many purple and silver-white garments of the nymph,
such as the holy dwellings of the blessed gods contain.
Then when he had searched the recesses of the great dwelling,
the son of Leto addressed glorious Hermes with these words:
"O child lying in the cradle, hurry up and tell me about the cows!
255 Else you and I will soon part not like two gentlemen.
I will cast you down and hurl you into gloomy Tartaros
and into dread and inescapable darkness; and neither your mother
nor your father will restore you to light but beneath the earth
you shall wander as lord of tiny babyfolk."
260 And Hermes addressed him with calculated words:
"Son of Leto, are not these harsh words you have spoken?
And are you here in search of roving cattle?
I have neither seen, nor found out, nor heard another man's word;
and I will neither tell, nor get the reward for telling.
265 I surely do not resemble a hardy rustler of cattle,
and this is no deed of mine, as I have cared for other matters:
I have cared for sleep, and milk from my mother's breast,
and for swaddling-clothes wrapped round my shoulders, and a warm bath.
May no one find out how this quarrel came to be!
270 For it would be a great wonder among the immortals
as to how a new-born baby through the doorway passed
with cattle dwelling in the fields; the claim is preposterous!
I was born yesterday, and the ground is rough for my tender feet.
If you wish, I will swear the great oath by my father's head.
275 I vow that I myself am not the culprit
and that I have seen no one else stealing your cows—
whatever these cows are; for I hear only rumors."
So he spoke and, with many a darting glance,
he moved his eyebrows up and down and looked hither and thither,
280 and with a long whistle he listened to the story as to an idle tale.
Far-shooting Apollon laughed gently and addressed him:
"Friend, I do think you are a scheming rogue,
and the way you talk you must often have bored your way
into well-built houses and stripped many men of their possessions,
285 as you quietly packed away their belongings.

You will be a pain to many shepherds dwelling outdoors
in mountain glades, when you come upon their herds of cattle
and fleecy sheep, driven by a craving for meat.
But come, lest this be your last and final sleep,
290 come down from the cradle, you comrade of dark night.
From now on you shall have this honor among the immortals,
to be called the chief of robbers all your days."
With these words Phoibos Apollon took up and carried the child.
And then mighty Argeiphontes pondered in himself
295 and, as he was lifted in Apollon's arms, sent forth an omen,
a hardy effort of the belly and a wreckless messenger.
And on top of that he swiftly sneezed, and Apollon
heard it and dropped glorious Hermes down on the ground.
And, although he was intent on his journey, he sat beside him
300 and chiding Hermes he addressed him with these words:
"Never fear, swathed child of Zeus and Maia.
Even later I shall find the precious cows
by these omens, and you shall lead the way."
So he spoke, and Kyllenian Hermes sprang up swiftly
305 and went in haste; he pushed back his ears with his hands
and, his swaddling clothes wrapped about his shoulders, he said:
"Whither are you carrying me, Far-Shooter, mightiest of all the gods?
Are you annoying me because you are so angry about the cows?
Oh my! I wish every single cow would perish!
310 Surely I neither stole the cows—whatever cows are—
nor saw another man do it. Rumor is all I hear!
Let Zeus Kronion be the judge and accept his verdict."
And after Hermes the shepherd and the glorious son of Leto
questioned each other on every point clearly
315 and still did not agree, [Apollon spoke] a truthful word.
. . . .
And not unjustly did he seize glorious Hermes for stealing
the cows, but the Kyllenian with wheedling words and artful tricks
wanted to deceive the Lord of the Silver Bow.
But when, though many were his own wiles, he found
320 Apollon full of devices, then he speedily led the way

across the sand, while the son of Zeus and Leto followed.
And the beautiful children of Zeus soon reached
the peak of fragrant Olympos and their father, Kronion;
for there the scales of justice were set for both.

325 A pleasant chatter permeated snowy Olympos
as ageless immortals gathered after golden-throned dawn.
Then Hermes and Apollon of the silver bow stood
before the knees of Zeus, and loud-thundering Zeus
spoke to his illustrious son and questioned him thus:

330 "Phoibos, whence are you bringing this welcome booty,
a new-born child who looks like a herald?
A weighty matter has come before the divine assembly."
Then the far-shooting lord, Apollon, answered him:
"Father, since you reproach me for being the only one

335 fond of booty, you shall soon hear no paltry tale.
After a long journey to the mountains of Kyllene
I found a child, a burgling looter
with sharpness of tongue such as I have seen in neither god
nor man, among those who cheat people on this earth.

340 He stole my cows from the meadow and drove them off;
he went along the shore of the resounding sea,
and headed straight for Pylos; there were monstrous footprints
of two kinds, such as are a noble god's wondrous works.
As for the cows, the black dust kept and showed

345 their footprints reversed in the direction of the flowery meadow.
And he himself—irrepressible fellow that he is—
walked over the sand neither on his feet nor on his hands.
But with some other contrivance he left such monstrous
tracks behind, as if one walked on slender oak-trees.

350 So long as he drove the cattle over sandy ground,
the tracks stood out clearly in the sand.
But when he came to the end of the great sandy stretch,
his own tracks and those of the cows became invisible
on the hard ground. But a mortal man observed him

355 as he drove the wide-browed kine straight to Pylos.
And after he had penned up the cows quietly

and, alternating roadsides, craftily made his way home,
he lay in his cradle, looking like the black night
in the darkness of the gloomy cave; and not even
360 a sharp-eyed eagle would have spotted him. With his hands
he rubbed his eyes and nursed wily thoughts,
and forthwith he uttered these reckless words:
'I have neither seen, nor found out, nor heard another man's word,
and I shall neither tell, nor get the reward for telling.' "
365 Phoibos Apollon spoke these words and then sat down.
But Hermes addressed Kronion, lord of all the gods,
and told the immortals quite another story:
"Father Zeus, I, indeed, shall speak the truth to you,
for I am all for the truth and know not how to lie.
370 He came to our place in search of his shambling cows
today, only a little after the sun had risen,
and brought none of the blessed gods as eyewitness or deponent.
He applied much force and ordered me to confess,
and often threatened to cast me down to broad Tartaros,
375 just because he is in the tender bloom of glorious youth
while I was born but yesterday; he knows all this himself,
for in no way do I resemble a hard man and a cattle-rustler.
Believe me—after all, you claim to be my dear father—
I did not drive his cows to my house and—bless me—
380 I did not cross over the threshold. This is the whole truth.
I greatly reverence Helios and the other gods,
and I love you and stand in awe of him. You do know
that I am not guilty, and now I take a great oath:
No! By these well-decked porticoes of the immortals!
385 Some day I will pay him back for this heartless inquiry,
stronger though he is; but do you help the younger."
Thus spoke Kyllenian Argeiphontes with a coy look
and held his swaddling clothes fast on his arm.
Zeus laughed out loud when he saw the mischievous child
390 denying so well and so adroitly any connection with the cattle.
He ordered them both to come to an accord
and search for the cattle, and Hermes to guide and lead the way

41

and in all good faith to show the place
where he had hidden away the precious cattle.
395 Then Kronides nodded with his head and illustrious Hermes obeyed,
for the mind of aegis-bearing Zeus easily commanded obedience.
And the beautiful children of Zeus both hurried away
to sandy Pylos and came to the ford of Alpheios.
They reached the fields and the high-roofed barn
400 where the beasts were tended at night-time.
Then Hermes went to the rocky cave
and drove out of it the precious cattle.
And Letoides looked aside and noticed the cowhides
on a steep rock, and immediately asked glorious Hermes:
405 "How could you, you clever rogue, have slaughtered two cows,
being still a new-born infant? Even I myself
look back and admire your strength; no need for you
to grow up for long, O Kyllenian son of Maia."
Thus he spoke, and with his hand he twisted mighty shackles
410 made of withes. But they swiftly took roots into the earth
and under his feet, as though grafted onto that spot,
and easily entwined each other and all the roving cows,
by the will of thievish Hermes, as Apollon
gazed in wonder. Then mighty Argeiphontes,
415 fire darting from his eyes, looked askance at the ground
. . . .
longing to hide. Then he easily soothed the far-shooting
son of glorious Leto, exactly as he wished,
mightier though Apollon was. Upon his left arm he took
the lyre and with the plectron struck it tunefully, and under his hand
420 it resounded awesomely. And Phoibos Apollon laughed
for joy as the lovely sound of the divine music
went through to his heart and sweet longing seized him
as he listened attentively. Playing sweetly on the lyre,
the son of Maia boldly stood to the left
425 of Phoibos Apollon and to the clear-sounding lyre
he sang as one sings preludes. His voice came out lovely,
and he sang of the immortal gods and of black earth,

how they came to be, and how each received his lot.
Of the gods with his song he first honored Mnemosyne,
430 mother of the Muses, for the son of Maia fell to her lot.
And the glorious son of Zeus honored the immortals
according to age, and as each one had been born,
singing of everything in due order as he played the lyre on his arm.
But a stubborn longing seized Apollon's heart in his breast,
435 and he spoke to him and addressed him with winged words:
"Scheming cattle-slayer, industrious comrade of the feast,
your performance is worth fifty cows;
I think we will settle our accounts at peace.
But come now, tell me this, inventive son of Maia:
440 Have these wondrous deeds followed you from birth,
or has some mortal man or deathless god
given you this glorious gift and taught you divine song?
Wondrous is this new-uttered sound I hear,
and such as I think no man or deathless god
445 dwelling on Olympos has ever yet learned,
except for you, O robber, son of Zeus and Maia.
What skill is this? What music for inescapable cares?
What virtuosity? For surely here are three things to take
all at once: good cheer, love, and sweet sleep.
450 I, too, am a follower of the Olympian Muses,
who cherish dance and the glorious field of song
and the festive chant and the lovely resonance of flutes.
But no display of skill by young men at feast
has ever touched my heart in this manner.
455 Son of Zeus, I marvel at your playing the lyre so charmingly.
Now, though you are little, since your ideas are remarkable,
sit down, friend, and have regard for the words of your elders.
There will indeed be renown for you among the immortals,
for you and your mother. I will speak concretely:
460 Yes, by the cornel spear, I shall truly make you
a glorious and thriving leader among the immortals,
and I shall give you splendid gifts without deception to the end."
And Hermes replied to him with calculated words:

43

"You question me carefully, Far-Shooter, and I
465   do not begrudge your becoming master of my skill.
You shall know it today. And I want to be gentle to you
in my words of advice—your mind knows all things well.
For, noble and mighty as you are, O son of Zeus, your seat
is first among the immortals, and wise Zeus loves you,
470   by every sacred right, and has granted you splendid gifts.
And they say, O Far-Shooter, that from Zeus and his divine voice
you learn the honors, the prophet's skills, and all god-given revelations.
I myself have learned that you have all these in abundance.
You may choose to learn whatever you desire,
475   but since your heart is so eager to play the lyre,
sing and play the lyre and minister to gay festivities,
receiving this skill from me and, friend, grant me glory.
Sing well with this clear-voiced mistress in your arms,
since you have the gift of beautiful and proper speech.
480   From now on in carefree spirit bring it to the well-provided feast,
the lovely dance, and the revel where men vie for glory,
as a fountain of good cheer day and night. Whoever
with skill and wisdom expertly asks, to him
it will speak and teach him all manner of things
485   joyful to the mind, being played with a gentle touch,
for it shuns toilsome practice. But if anyone should
in ignorance question it at first with rudeness,
to him in vain it will chatter high-flown gibberish forever.
You may choose to learn whatever you desire;
490   and I will make a gift of it to you, glorious son of Zeus.
For my part, O Far-Shooter, I will graze the roving cattle
on the pastures of the mountain and the horse-nurturing plain,
where the cows are mounted by the bulls to give birth
to males and females at random. And though your mind
495   is set on profit, there is no need for you to rage with anger."
With these words he offered him the lyre, and Phoibos Apollon took it,
and put in Hermes' hand a shining whip,
and commanded him to be a cowherd. The son of Maia accepted
joyfully. And the glorious son of Leto, far-shooting

500   lord Apollon upon his left arm took the lyre
and struck it tunefully with the plectron. It resounded
awesomely under his hand, and the god sang to it beautifully.
Then both of them turned the cows toward
the divine meadow, and the beautiful children of Zeus
505   rushed to return to snowy Olympos,
delighting in the lyre; and thus wise Zeus rejoiced
and brought them together in friendship. For his part, Hermes
always loved the son of Leto as he does even now,
and he gave the lovely lyre as a token
510   to the Far-Shooter, who played it on his arm expertly.
And Hermes again invented the skill of a new art,
for he made the resounding pipes which can be heard from afar.
And then the son of Leto addressed Hermes thus:
"Son of Maia, crafty guide, I fear you might
515   steal back my lyre and the curved bow.
For it is your Zeus-given prerogative to tend to
barter among the men of this nourishing earth;
but if you would deign to swear the great oath of the gods,
either by a nod of your head, or by the potent water of the Styx,
520   your deeds would be gracious and dear to my heart."
And then the son of Maia with a nod of his head promised
never to steal away whatever the Far-Shooter possessed,
and never to approach his sturdy house. Then Apollon,
the son of Leto, for the love of Hermes' friendship, vowed
525   that no one else among the immortals to him would be dearer,
neither god, nor man descended from Zeus. And a perfect

. . . .

"an omen among all the immortals I shall make [you],
one honored and trusted by my heart. And later
I shall give you a beautiful staff of wealth and prosperity,
530   a golden one with three branches, to protect you against harm
and to accomplish all the laws of noble words and deeds,
which I profess to know from the voice of Zeus.
Mightiest one and cherished by Zeus, it is not the divine will
for you or any other immortal to know the divination

535 you are asking about. The mind of Zeus knows this. For my part,
I pledged and agreed and then swore a mighty oath
that, except for me, none of the eternal gods
would know the inscrutable will of Zeus.
And you, my brother of the golden wand, do not ask me
540 to show the divine decrees which far-seeing Zeus contemplates.
To some men I will bring harm and to others benefit
as I herd the wretched tribes of men about.
My utterance will bring blessings to those who come
guided by the voice and flight of birds of sure omen.
545 No deception for him; he will profit from what I utter.
But whoever puts faith in the idle chatter of birds
and wishes to pry into my divination, against my designs,
and to understand more than the eternal gods,
makes his journey in vain; yet his gifts I shall take.
550 And now, son of glorious Maia and of Zeus who holds
the aegis, helpful genius of the gods, I will tell you
another thing: there are three awesome sisters,
virgins, delighting in their swift wings.
Their heads are besprinkled with white barley flour,
555 and they dwell under the fold of Parnassos,
apart from me, as teachers of divination, which I studied
when as a mere child I tended the cows, and my father
did not mind. From there flying now here, now there,
they feed on honeycomb and bring each thing to pass.
560 And after they eat yellow honey, they are seized
with mantic frenzy and are eager to speak the truth.
But if they are robbed of the sweet food of the gods,
then they do buzz about in confusion and lie.
These, then, I give you, and do you question them exactly,
565 and delight your heart; and if you are a mortal man's teacher,
he will often listen to you if good fortune is his.
Keep these, son of Maia, and the roving, curved-horned cattle
and tend horses and hardy mules."
[He commanded] glorious Hermes to be lord over
570 lions with flashing eyes and boars with gleaming tusks,

and dogs, and all herds, and sheep nurtured by the broad earth;
and to be appointed sole messenger to Hades,
who, though implacable, will give no small prize.
Thus lord Apollon showed his love for the son of Maia
75 with every kind of affection. And Kronion bestowed grace upon him.
He is a companion to all immortals and mortals.
Little is the profit he brings, and he beguiles endlessly
the tribes of mortal men throughout the night.
And so, farewell, son of Zeus and Maia;
80 but I shall remember you and another song, too.

5. TO APHRODITE

1 Sing to me, O Muse, of the works of golden Aphrodite,
the Cyprian, who stirs sweet longing in gods
and subdues the races of mortal men as well as
the birds that swoop from the sky and all the beasts
5 that are nurtured in their multitudes on both land and sea.
Indeed all have concern for the works of fair-wreathed Kythereia.
Three are the minds which she can neither sway nor deceive:
first is the daughter of aegis-bearing Zeus, gray-eyed Athena.
The works of Aphrodite the golden bring no pleasure to her,
10 but she finds joy in wars and in the work of Ares
and in the strife of battle and in tending to deeds of splendor.
She was first to teach the craftsmen of this earth
how to make carriages and chariots with intricate patterns of bronze.
And she taught lustrous works to soft-skinned maidens
15 in their houses, placing skill in each one's mind.
Second is hallooing Artemis of the golden shafts,
whom smile-loving Aphrodite can never tame in love.
For she delights in the bow and in slaying mountain beasts,
in the lyre and the dance and in shrill cries
20 and in shaded groves and in the city of just men.
Third is a revered maiden not charmed by the deeds of Aphrodite,

47

Hestia, whom Kronos of crooked counsels begat first
and youngest too, by the will of aegis-bearing Zeus.
Poseidon and Apollon courted this mighty goddess
25 but she was unwilling and constantly refused.
She touched the head of aegis-bearing Zeus
and swore a great oath, which has been brought to pass,
that she, the illustrious goddess, would remain a virgin forever.
Instead of marriage Zeus the Father gave her a fair prize,
30 and she took the choicest boon and sat in the middle of the house.
In all the temples of the gods she has her share of honor
and for all mortals she is of all the gods the most venerated.
Of these three she can neither sway the mind, nor deceive them.
But none of the others, neither blessed god
35 nor mortal man, has escaped Aphrodite.
She even led astray the mind of Zeus who delights in thunder
and who is the greatest and has the highest honor.
Even his wise mind she tricks when she wills it
and easily mates him with mortal women,
40 making him forget Hera, his wife and sister,
by far the most beautiful among the deathless goddesses
and the most illustrious child to issue from crafty Kronos
and mother Rhea. And Zeus, knower of indestructible plans,
made her his modest and prudent wife.
45 But even in Aphrodite's soul Zeus placed sweet longing
to mate with a mortal man; his purpose was that even she
might not be kept away from a mortal's bed for long,
and that some day the smile-loving goddess might not
laugh sweetly and boast among all the gods
50 of how she had joined in love gods to mortal women,
who bore mortal sons to the deathless gods,
and of how she had paired goddesses with mortal men.
And so he placed in her heart sweet longing for Anchises
who then, looking like an immortal in body,
55 tended cattle on the towering mountains of Ida, rich in springs.
When indeed smile-loving Aphrodite saw him,
she fell in love with him, and awesome longing seized her heart.

She went to Cyprus and entered her redolent temple
at Paphos, where her precinct and balmy temple are.
60 There she entered and behind her closed the shining doors;
and there the Graces bathed her and annointed her
with ambrosian oil such as is rubbed on deathless gods,
divinely sweet, and made fragrant for her sake.
After she clothed her body with beautiful garments
65 and decked herself with gold, smile-loving Aphrodite
left sweet-smelling Cyprus behind and rushed toward Troy,
moving swiftly on a path high up in the clouds.
And she reached Ida, rich in springs, mother of beasts,
and over the mountain she made straight for the stalls.
70 And along with her, fawning, dashed gray wolves
and lions with gleaming eyes and bears and swift leopards,
ever hungry for deer. And when she saw them, she was delighted
in her heart and placed longing in their breasts,
so that they lay together in pairs along the shady glens.
75 But she herself reached the well-built shelters
and found the hero Anchises, whose beauty was divine,
left alone and away from the others, by the stalls.
All the others followed the cattle on the grassy pastures,
but he was left alone by the stalls, and away from the others
80 he moved about and played a loud and clear lyre.
And Aphrodite, the daughter of Zeus, stood before him,
in size and form like an unwed maiden,
so that he might not see who she was and be afraid.
When Anchises saw her, he pondered and marveled
85 at her size and form, and at her glistening garments.
She was clothed in a robe more brilliant than gleaming fire
and wore spiral bracelets and shining earrings,
while round her tender neck there were beautiful necklaces,
lovely, golden and of intricate design. Like the moon's
90 was the radiance round her soft breasts, a wonder to the eye.
Desire seized Anchises, and to her he uttered these words:
"Lady, welcome to this house, whoever of the blessed ones you are:
whether you are Artemis, or Leto, or golden Aphrodite,

or well-born Themis, or gray-eyed Athena,
95 or yet perchance one of the Graces, who with all
the gods keep company and are called immortal,
or one of the nymphs who haunt these beautiful woods,
or one of the nymphs who dwell on this beautiful mountain
and in the springs of rivers and the grassy dells.
100 Upon a lofty peak, which can be seen from all around,
I shall make you an altar and offer you fair sacrifices
in all seasons. And with kindly heart grant me
to be an eminent man among the Trojans,
to leave flourishing offspring behind me,
105 and to live long and behold the light of the sun,
prospering among the people, and so reach the threshold of old age."
And then Aphrodite, the daughter of Zeus, answered him:
"Anchises, most glorious of all men born on earth,
I surely am no goddess; why do you liken me to the immortals?
110 A mortal am I, and born of a mortal woman.
Renowned Otreus is my father—have you perchance heard his name?—
who is lord over all of well-fortified Phrygia.
And I know well both my language and yours,
for a Trojan nurse reared me in my house; she took me
115 from my dear mother and devotedly cherished me when I was little.
For this reason indeed I know your language too.
But now Argeiphontes of the golden wand carried me off
from the dance of hallooing Artemis of the golden shafts.
Many of us nymphs and maidens, worth many cows to their parents,
120 were playing, and endless was the crowd encircling us.
From there Argeiphontes of the golden wand abducted me
and carried me over many works of mortal men,
over much undivided and uninhabited land, where beasts
which eat raw flesh roam through the shady glens,
125 and I thought that my feet would never again touch the life-giving earth.
He said I should be called your wedded wife, Anchises,
and sharing your bed would bear you fine children.
But when mighty Argeiphontes had shown and explained this to me,
again he went away among the tribes of the immortals;

130   and so I am before you because my need is compelling.
By Zeus I beseech you and by your noble parents,
for base ones could not bear offspring like you.
Take me untouched and innocent of love
and show me to your father and wise mother
135   and to your brothers born of the same womb;
I shall be no unseemly daughter and sister.
Quickly send a messenger to the Phrygians, who have swift horses,
to bring word to my father and to my mother in her grief;
they will send you much gold and many woven garments,
140   and do you accept all these splendid rewards.
Once these things are done, prepare the lovely marriage feast,
which is honored by both men and immortal gods."
With these words the goddess placed sweet desire in his heart,
so that love seized Anchises and he addressed her:
145   "If you are mortal and born of a mortal woman
and Otreus is your father, famous by name, as you say,
and if you are come here by the will of Hermes,
the immortal guide, you shall be called my wife forever.
And so neither god nor mortal man will restrain me
150   till I have mingled with you in love
right now; not even if far-shooting Apollon himself
should shoot grievous arrows from his silver bow.
O godlike woman, willingly would I go to the house of Hades
once I have climbed into your bed."
155   With these words he took her by the hand; and smile-loving Aphrodite,
turning her face away, with beautiful eyes downcast, went coyly
to the well-made bed, which was already laid
with soft coverings for its lord.
On it were skins of bears and deep-roaring lions,
160   which he himself had killed on the high mountains.
And when they climbed onto the well-wrought bed,
first Anchises took off the bright jewels from her body,
brooches, spiral bracelets, earrings and necklaces,
and loosed her girdle, and her brilliant garments
165   he stripped off and laid upon a silver-studded seat.

Then by the will of the gods and destiny he, a mortal,
lay beside an immortal, not knowing what he did.
And at the hour shepherds turn their oxen and goodly sheep
back to the stalls from the flowering pastures,
170   she poured sweet sleep over Anchises
and clothed her body in her beautiful clothes.
When the noble goddess had clothed her body in beautiful clothes,
she stood by the couch; her head touched the well-made roof-beam
and her cheeks were radiant with divine beauty,
175   such as belongs to fair-wreathed Kythereia.
Then she roused him from sleep and addressed him thus:
"Arise, Dardanides! Why do you sleep so deeply?
And consider whether I look the same
as when you first saw me with your eyes."
180   So she spoke. And he, arising from sleep, obeyed her forthwith.
And when he saw Aphrodite's neck and lovely eyes,
he was seized with fear and turned his eyes aside.
Then with his cloak his handsome face he covered
and spoke to her winged words in prayer:
185   "Goddess, as soon as I saw you with my eyes
I knew that you were divine; but you did not tell the truth.
Yet by aegis-bearing Zeus I beseech you
not to let me live impotent among men,
but have mercy on me; for the man who lies
190   with immortal goddesses is not left unharmed."
And Aphrodite the daughter of Zeus answered him:
"Anchises, most glorious of mortal men,
courage! Have little fear in your heart.
No need to be afraid that you may suffer harm from me
195   or from the other blessed ones, for by the gods you are loved.
And you shall have a dear son who will rule among the Trojans,
and to his offspring children shall always be born.
Aineias his name shall be, because I was seized
by awful grief for sharing a mortal man's bed.
200   But of all mortal men your race is always
closest to the gods in looks and stature.

Wise Zeus abducted fair-haired Ganymedes
for his beauty, to be among the immortals
and pour wine for the gods in the house of Zeus,
205   a marvel to look upon, honored by all the gods,
as from the golden bowl he draws red nectar.
Relentless grief seized the heart of Tros, nor did he know
whither the divine whirlwind had carried off his dear son.
So thereafter he wept for him unceasingly;
210   and Zeus pitied him and gave him high-stepping horses,
such as carry the immortals, as reward for his son.
He gave them as a gift for him to have, and guiding
Argeiphontes at the behest of Zeus told him in detail
how his son would be immortal and ageless like the gods.
215   And when he heard Zeus' message,
he no longer wept but rejoiced in his heart
and was gladly carried by the careering horses.
So, too, golden-throned Eos abducted Tithonos,
one of your own race, who resembled the immortals.
220   She went to ask Kronion, lord of dark clouds,
that he should be immortal and live forever.
And Zeus nodded assent to her and fulfilled her wish.
Mighty Eos was too foolish to think of asking
youth for him and to strip him of baneful old age.
225   Indeed, so long as much-coveted youth was his,
he took his delight in early-born, golden-throned Eos,
and dwelt by the stream of Okeanos at the ends of the earth.
But when the first gray hairs began to flow down
from his comely head and noble chin,
230   mighty Eos did refrain from his bed,
though she kept him in her house and pampered him
with food and ambrosia and gifts of fine clothing.
But when detested old age weighed heavy on him
and he could move or lift none of his limbs,
235   this is the counsel that to her seemed best in her heart:
she placed him in a chamber and shut its shining doors.
His voice flows endlessly and there is no strength,

such as there was before, in his crooked limbs.
If this were to be your lot among immortals, I should not choose
240 for you immortality and eternal life.
But should you live on such as you now are
in looks and build, and be called my husband,
then no grief would enfold my prudent heart.
But now you will soon be enveloped by leveling old age,
245 that pitiless companion of every man,
baneful, wearisome, and hated even by the gods.
But great shame shall be mine among the immortal gods
to the end of all time because of you.
Till now they feared my scheming tattle,
250 by which, soon or late, I mated all immortal gods
to mortal women, for my will tamed them all.
But now my mouth will not bear to mention this
among the immortals because, struck by great madness
in a wretched and grave way, and driven out of my mind,
255 I mated with a mortal and put a child beneath my girdle.
As soon as this child sees the light of the sun,
the full-bosomed mountain nymphs who dwell
on this great and holy mountain will nurture him.
They do not take after either mortals or immortals;
260 they live long and eat immortal food,
and among the immortals they move nimbly in the beautiful dance.
The Seilenoi and sharp-eyed Argeiphontes
mingle with them in love in caves where desire lurks.
When they are born, firs and towering oaks
265 spring up on the man-nourishing earth
and grow into lush beauty on the high mountains.
They stand lofty, and are called sanctuaries
of the gods; and mortals do not fell them with the ax.
But whenever fated death is near at hand,
270 first these beautiful trees wither on their ground,
the bark all around them shrivels up, the branches fall away,
and their souls and those of the nymphs leave the light of the sun together.
They will keep my son and nurture him.

As soon as he reaches much-coveted adolescence,
275   the goddesses will bring the child here to show him to you.
And, to tell you all I have in mind,
toward the fifth year I will come and bring my son.
And when you first lay your eyes upon this blossom,
you will delight in the sight, for so much like a god he will be;
280   and you shall take him forthwith to windy Ilion.
But if any mortal man should ask you
what sort of mother carried your dear son under her girdle,
do remember to speak to him as I bid you:
'He is the son, they say, of a nymph with a petal-soft face,
285   one of those who dwell on this forest-covered mountain.'
But if you reveal this and boast with foolish heart
to have mingled in love with fair-wreathed Kythereia,
an angry Zeus will smite you with a smoking thunderbolt.
I have told you everything; with this clear in your mind,
290   refrain from naming me, and heed divine anger."
With these words she darted up to the windy sky.
Hail, O goddess and queen of cultivated Cyprus!
I began with you but now shall go to another hymn.

6. TO APHRODITE

Of august gold-wreathed and beautiful Aphrodite
I shall sing, to whose domain belong the battlements
of all sea-laved Cyprus where, blown by the moist breath of Zephyros,
she was carried over the waves of the resounding sea
5   in soft foam. The gold-filleted Horae
happily welcomed her and clothed her with heavenly raiment.
Then on her divine head they placed a well-wrought crown,
beautiful and golden, and in her pierced ears
flowers of brass and precious gold.
10   Round her tender neck and silver-white breasts
they decked her with golden necklaces such as the gold-filleted

Horae themselves are adorned with whenever they go
to lovely dances of the gods and to their father's house.
And after they decked her body with every sort of jewel,
15 they brought her to the immortals, who saw and welcomed her,
giving her their hands, and each one wished
that he might take her home as his wedded wife;
for they marveled at the looks of violet-crowned Kythereia.
Hail, honey-sweet goddess with the fluttering eyelids!
20 Grant me victory in this contest and arrange my song.
And I shall remember you and another song, too.

7. TO DIONYSOS

I shall recall to mind how Dionysos, son of glorious Semele,
appeared by the shore of the barren sea
on a jutting headland, looking like a young man
in the first bloom of manhood. His beautiful dark hair
5 danced about him, and on his stout shoulders he wore
a purple cloak. Soon on a well-benched ship
pirates moved forward swiftly on the wine-dark sea;
they were Tyrsenians led by an evil doom. When they saw him
they signaled to each other and then leapt out and quickly seized him
10 and put him on board their ship, glad in their hearts.
For they thought he was the son of a Zeus-cherished king
and wanted to bind him with painful shackles.
But the shackles could not hold him and the withes fell far away
from his hands and feet; and he sat there smiling
15 with his dark eyes. And when the helmsman perceived what this meant,
forthwith he called upon his shipmates and said:
"Why do you seize and bind this mighty god, you crazy men?
Our well-made ship cannot even carry him!
He is either Zeus or Apollon of the silver bow,
20 or Poseidon, for he looks not like mortal men
but like the gods who have their homes on Olympos.

But come! Let us leave him upon the black mainland
at once! And do not lay hands on him lest he be angered
and raise violent winds and a great storm."
25 So he spoke, but the captain scolded him with harsh words:
"Madman! Keep your mind on the tail wind, and hold all the lines
and hoist the sail of the ship. The men will take care of him.
I reckon Egypt or Cyprus is his destination
or the Hyperboreans or yet some more distant land.
30 When we are through with him he will talk and tell about his friends
and brothers, and all his goods, since some god has sent him our way."
This said, he hoisted mast and sail on the ship,
and the wind blew the mainsail full as they pulled the lines
tight on both sides. But soon wondrous deeds unfolded before their eyes:
35 first throughout the swift black ship sweet and fragrant wine
formed a gurgling stream and a divine smell
arose as all the crew watched in mute wonder.
And next on the topmost sail a vine spread about
all over, and many grapes were hanging down
40 in clusters. Then round the mast dark ivy twined,
luxuriant with flowers and lovely growing berries;
the thole-pins were crowned with wreaths. When they saw this
they bade the helmsman put the ship to shore.
Now the god became a fearsome, loud-roaring lion
45 in the bow of the ship and then amidships
a shaggy bear he caused to appear as a portent.
The bear reared with fury and the lion scowled dreadfully
on the topmost bench. The crew hastened in fear to the stern
and stood dumbfounded round the helmsman,
50 a man of prudent mind, as the lion swiftly lunged
upon the captain and seized him. When they saw this,
they escaped evil fate by jumping overboard into the shining sea
and turning into dolphins. But, pitying the helmsman,
the god held him back and made him most happy with these words:
55 "Courage! . . . you are dear to my heart.
I am loud-roaring Dionysos, born of the daughter of Kadmos,
Semele, who mingled in love with Zeus."

Hail, child of Semele with the fair face! There is no way
one can forget you and still compose sweet songs.

8. TO ARES

Mighty Ares, golden-helmeted rider of chariots,
stout-hearted, shield-carrying and bronze-geared savior of cities,
strong-handed and unwearying lord of the spear, bulwark of Olympos,
father of fair Victory, and succorer of Themis.
5   You curb the unruly and lead truly just men,
O paragon of manly excellence, wheeling your luminous orb
through the seven-pathed constellations of the sky, where flaming
steeds ever carry you above the third heavenly arch.
Hearken, helper of mortals and giver of flourishing youth,
10 and from above shine a gentle light on my life
and my martial prowess, that I may be able
to ward off bitter cowardice from my head,
to bend wisely my soul's beguiling impulse
and to restrain the sharp fury of my heart, whenever
15 it provokes me to enter chilling battle. But, O blessed one,
give me courage to stay within the secure laws of peace
and to escape the enemy's charge and a violent death.

9. TO ARTEMIS

Sing, O Muse, of Artemis, sister of the Far-darter,
arrow-pouring virgin, who was nurtured with Apollon.
She waters her horses by Meles with its tall rushes
and thence on her golden chariot through Smyrna courses
5 to Klaros, rich in vineyards, where Apollon of the silver bow
sits waiting for the far-shooting arrow-pourer.
You and all goddesses, farewell and delight in my song!

But I shall start my song with you
and then shall go to another hymn.

10. TO APHRODITE

I shall sing of Kythereia, born on Cyprus,
who brings sweet gifts to mortals, and whose lovely face
ever smiles radiant with lambent beauty on it.
Hail, goddess and mistress of well-built Salamis
5   and of sea-laved Cyprus! Grant me enchanting song.
And now I will remember you and another song, too.

11. TO ATHENA

I begin to sing of Pallas Athena, defender of cities,
awesome goddess; she and Ares care for deeds of war,
cities being sacked and cries of battle.
And she protects an army going to war and returning.
5   Hail, O goddess, and grant me good fortune and happiness.

12. TO HERA

Of golden-throned Hera I sing, born of Rhea,
queen of the gods, unexcelled in beauty,
sister and glorious wife of loud-thundering Zeus.
All the gods on lofty Olympos reverence her
5   and honor her together with Zeus who delights in thunder.

13. TO DEMETER

Of Demeter, the lovely-haired and august goddess,
and of her daughter, the fair Persephone, I begin to sing.
Hail, O goddess! Keep this city safe, and guide my song.

14. TO THE MOTHER OF THE GODS

Sing to me, O Muse, clear-voiced daughter of great Zeus,
of the mother of all gods and of all men.
In the din of rattles and drums and in the sound of pipes
she delights. In the howl of wolves and the roar of glaring lions,
5 in resounding mountains and wooded glens she finds her joy.
Farewell! And you and all the goddesses delight in my song.

15. TO LION-HEARTED HERAKLES

I shall sing of Zeus' son, Herakles, noblest of mortals,
born at Thebes, city of lovely dances,
of the union of Alkmene with Zeus, lord of dark clouds.
In the past he wandered endlessly over the boundless earth and sea
5 on missions ordered by lord Eurystheus,
and he committed many reckless deeds and himself endured many.
But now he joyously dwells in his beautiful abode
on snowy Olympos with fair-ankled Hebe as his spouse.
Hail, O lord and son of Zeus! Grant me virtue and happiness.

16. TO ASKLEPIOS

I begin to sing of Asklepios, healer of diseases
and son of Apollon. Noble Koronis, daughter of

King Phlegyas bore him on the plain of Dotion,
to be a great joy for men and charm evil pains away.
5   And so hail to you, O lord! I pray to you in my song.

17. TO THE DIOSKOUROI

Sing, O clear-voiced Muse, of Kastor and Polydeukes,
the Tyndaridai, whom Olympian Zeus begot
and mighty Leda bore beneath the peaks of Taygetos,
having secretly succumbed to the passion of Zeus, lord of dark clouds.
5   Hail O Tyndaridai, riders of swift horses!

18. TO HERMES

I sing of Hermes, the Kyllenian Argeiphontes,
who is lord of Kyllene and of Arcadia abounding with sheep.
This helpful messenger of the gods was born of the amorous union
of the bashful daughter of Atlas with Zeus.
5   She shunned the company of the blessed gods
and dwelt in a deep-shaded cave, where Kronion
lay with the fair-tressed nymph in the dead of night,
while sweet sleep overcame white-armed Hera;
thus he escaped the eyes of both gods and mortal men.
10   So Hail, son of Zeus and Maia!
I began with you, but I will now turn to another hymn.
Hail, Hermes, guide and giver of things graceful and good!

19. TO PAN

Sing to me, O Muse, of Hermes' dear child,
the goat-footed, two-horned, din-loving one, who roams

over wooded glades together with dance-loving nymphs;
they tread on the peaks of sheer cliffs,
5   calling upon Pan, the splendid-haired and unkempt
god of shepherds, to whose domain all the snowy hills
and mountain peaks and rocky paths fall.
He wanders all over through the thick brushwood,
now drawn to gently flowing streams,
10   now again making his way through to steep crags
and climbing to the topmost peak overlooking the flocks.
Many times he careers through chalk-white, lofty mountains
and many times he drives beasts onto jutting rocks
and, his keen eye fixed on them, he slays them. Then only at evening
15   he shouts as he returns from the hunt and on his pipes of reed
he gently plays sweet music. In song he could even outdo
that bird which sits among the leaves at flower-rich springtime
and, pouring forth its dirge, trills honey-voiced tunes.
With him at that time are the clear-voiced mountain nymphs,
20   dancing with swift feet and singing at some dark spring,
as the echo moans about the mountain peak.
The god glides now here, now there and then to the middle of the dance,
setting the pace with quick feet. On his back he wears
a bay lynx-skin as his heart delights in the shrill songs
25   in a soft meadow where the crocus and the fragrant hyacinth
blossom forth and entwine with the grass in fast embrace.
They sing of the blessed gods and of lofty Olympos
and, above all others, they tell of helpful Hermes,
how he is the swift messenger to all the gods
30   and how he came to the mother of flocks, Arcadia, abounding in springs,
where there is a sacred precinct for him as god of Kyllene.
There, though he was a god, he tended curly-fleeced sheep
for a mortal man, because there came upon him and grew strong
a melting desire to mingle in love with the fair-tressed daughter
of Dryops.
35   His was a festive wedding, and inside the house she bore
to Hermes a dear son, from birth monstrous to behold,
with goat's feet and two horns, boisterous and sweet-laughing.

His mother sprang up and fled; the nurse in turn left the child behind
because she was afraid when she saw his wild and well-bearded visage.
40 Helpful Hermes quickly received him into his arms,
and in his divine heart the joy overflowed.
He wrapped the child in snug skins of mountain hares
and swiftly went to the abodes of the immortals.
He then set him down beside Zeus and the other gods
45 and showed them his boy: all of them were delighted
in their hearts and Bacchic Dionysos above all others.
They called him Pan because he cheered the hearts of all.
And so hail to you, O lord! I propitiate you with song.
And now I shall remember you and another song, too.

20. TO HEPHAISTOS

Sing, O clear-voiced Muse, of Hephaistos renowned for skill,
who along with gray-eyed Athena taught fine crafts
to men of this earth; indeed before that time
they used to live in mountain caves like wild beasts.
5 But now, thanks to Hephaistos, the famous craftsman,
they have learned crafts and easily for the full year
they lead a carefree existence in their own homes.
But have mercy on me, Hephaistos, and grant me virtue and happiness.

21. TO APOLLON

Phoibos, of you even the crying swan sings to flapping wings
as it swoops down upon the bank of the eddying river
Peneios. And of you the sweet-singing bard ever sings
first and last with his high-tuned lyre.
5 And so hail to you, O lord! I propitiate you with my song.

22. TO POSEIDON

I begin to sing of Poseidon, the great god,
mover of the earth and of the barren sea,
the sea-god who is lord of Helikon and broad Aigai.
O Earth-shaker, two-fold is your god-given prerogative,
5   to be a tamer of horses and a savior of ships.
Hail, Poseidon, black-maned holder of the earth!
Have a kindly heart, O blessed one, and come to the aid of sailors!

23. TO ZEUS

I shall sing of Zeus, the best and the greatest of gods,
far-seeing, mighty, fulfiller of designs who confides
his tight-knit schemes to Themis as she sits leaning upon him.
Have mercy, far-seeing Kronides, most glorious and great!

24. TO HESTIA

Hestia, you who tend the sacred dwelling
of the far-shooting lord, Apollon, at holy Pytho,
from your tresses flowing oil ever drips down.
Come to this house! Come in gentle spirit
5   with resourceful Zeus and grant grace to my song!

25. TO THE MUSES AND APOLLON

Let me begin with the Muses and Apollon and Zeus,
because it is through the Muses and far-shooting Apollon
that singers and lyre-players exist upon the earth;

kings are from Zeus. Blessed is the man whom the Muses
5   love, for sweet speech flows from his mouth.
Hail, children of Zeus! Do honor my song!
And I shall remember you and another song, too.

26. TO DIONYSOS

I begin to sing of boisterous Dionysos of the ivy-wreathed head,
the noble son of Zeus and glorious Semele.
The lovely-haired nymphs nurtured him and from his lordly father
took him to their bosoms to cuddle and nurse
5   in the dells of Nysa. He grew up by his father's will
inside a sweet-smelling cave as one of the immortals.
But after the goddesses brought him up with many songs,
covered with ivy and laurel he started
haunting the wooded glens. The nymphs followed him
10   and he led the way as the boundless forest resounded with din.
And so hail to you, Dionysos, with your many grapes!
Grant that we joyously reach this season again
and then after this season many more years.

27. TO ARTEMIS

I sing of Artemis of the golden shafts, the modest maiden
who loves the din of the hunt and shoots volleys of arrows at stags.
She is the twin sister of Apollon of the golden sword,
and through shady mountains and windy peaks
5   she delights in the chase as she stretches her golden bow
to shoot the bitter arrows. The crests of tall mountains
tremble, and the thick-shaded forest resounds
dreadfully with the cries of beasts, while the earth
and the fishy deep shudder. Hers is a mighty heart,

10 and she roams all over destroying the brood of wild beasts.
But when the arrow-pouring goddess who spots the wild beasts
has taken her pleasure and delighted her mind, after slacking
the well-taut bow, she comes to the great house of her dear brother,
Phoibos Apollon, to the opulent district of Delphi,
15 to set up a beautiful dance of the Muses and the Graces.
There she hangs her resilient bow and her arrows,
and wearing her graceful jewelry, she is their leader
in the dance. Divine is the sound they utter
as they sing of how fair-ankled Leto gave birth to children,
20 who among the gods are by far the best in deed and counsel.
Hail, O children of Zeus and lovely-haired Leto!
I shall remember you and another song, too.

28. TO ATHENA

I begin to sing of Pallas Athena, the glorious goddess,
gray-eyed, resourceful, of implacable heart.
This bashful maiden is a mighty defender of cities,
the Tritogeneia, whom Zeus the counselor himself
5 bore from his august head, clad with golden and resplendent
warlike armor, as awe lay hold of all the immortal
onlookers. And before Zeus the aegis-holder
she sprang swiftly from his immortal head,
brandishing a sharp-pointed spear. Great Olympos quaked
10 dreadfully under the might of the gray-eyed goddess, as the earth
all about resounded awesomely, and the sea moved
and heaved with purple waves. The briny sea calmed down
when the splendid son of Hyperion stopped
his fleet-footed horses long enough for maidenly
15 Pallas Athena to take from her immortal shoulders
the divine weapons. And Zeus the counselor exulted.
And so hail to you, O child of aegis-holding Zeus!
I shall remember you and another song, too.

29. TO HESTIA

Hestia, in the lofty dwellings of all,
both of immortal gods and of men who walk on the earth,
you have attained an eternal abode and the highest honor,
together with a fair and honorific prize: for without you
5 there can be no feasts for mortals, if at the beginning
yours is not the first and last libation of honey-sweet wine.
And you, Argeiphontes, son of Zeus and Maia,
messenger of the blessed gods, golden-staffed giver of things good,
dwell [with Hestia] in beautiful houses, with loving hearts

. . . .

10 Be favorable and help, both you and reverend and dear
Hestia. Since both of you know the good works
of the men of this earth, accompany them with youthful mind.
Hail, O daughter of Kronos, both you and Hermes of the golden wand!
I shall remember you and another song, too.

30. TO EARTH, MOTHER OF ALL

I shall sing of well-formed Earth, mother of all
and oldest of all, who nourishes all things living on land.
Her beauty nurtures all creatures that walk upon the land,
and all that move in the deep or fly in the air.
5 O mighty one, you are the source of fair children and goodly fruit,
and on you it depends to give life to, or take it away from,
mortal men. Blessed is the man you favor
with willing heart, for he will have everything in abundance.
His life-giving land teems with crops, and on his fields
10 his flocks thrive while his house is filled with goods.
Such men with just laws rule a city
of beautiful women, while much prosperity and wealth attend them.
Their sons glory in youthful glee
and their daughters with cheerful hearts in flower-dances

15　play and frisk over soft flowers of the field.
　　These are the ones you honor, O revered goddess of plenty!
　　Hail, mother of the gods and wife of starry Ouranos!
　　For my song do grant me livelihood that gladdens the heart,
　　and I shall remember you and another song, too.

31. TO HELIOS

O Muse Kalliope, begin to sing again
of brilliant Helios whom cow-eyed Euryphaëssa
bore to the son of Ge and starry Ouranos.
For Hyperion married his own sister, the glorious
5　Euryphaëssa, who bore him beautiful children:
　　rosy-armed Eos, fair-tressed Selene
　　and tireless Helios, so much like the immortals;
　　he shines his light on both men and immortal gods
　　as he rides his horses. With his eyes he gazes fiercely
10　from his golden helmet, while his luminous rays
　　glisten brilliantly and the shining cheek-pieces
　　descend from his head over his temples and border his graceful
　　and effulgent face. On his skin a beautiful and finely woven
　　garment shimmers as the winds blow, and his stallions
　　. . . . .
15　After he stays his golden-yoked chariot and horses there,
　　he wondrously sends them to the ocean through the sky.
　　Hail, O lord! Kindly grant me livelihood that gladdens the heart.
　　Starting with you I shall glorify the race of mortal men,
　　the demigods whose deeds the gods have showed to men.

32. TO SELENE

Muses, sweet-speaking daughters of Zeus Kronides
and mistresses of song, sing next of long-winged Moon!

From her immortal head a heaven-sent glow
envelops the earth and great beauty arises
5 under its radiance. From her golden crown the dim air
is made to glitter as her rays turn night to noon,
whenever bright Selene, having bathed her beautiful skin
in the Ocean, put on her shining raiment
and harnessed her proud-necked and glistening steeds,
10 swiftly drives them on as their manes play
with the evening, dividing the months. Her great orbit is full
and as she waxes a most brilliant light appears
in the sky. Thus to mortals she is a sign and a token.
Once Kronides shared her bed and her love;
15 she became pregnant and gave birth to Pandeia,
a maiden outstanding for beauty among the immortal gods.
Hail, queen and white-armed goddess, splendid Selene,
kindly and fair-tressed! Beginning with you I shall sing
of the glories of demigods, whose deeds are ennobled by bards,
20 who serve the Muses with their lovely mouths.

33. TO THE DIOSKOUROI

Quick-glancing Muses, sing of Zeus' sons,
the Tyndaridai, splendid children of fair-ankled Leda,
horse-taming Kastor and blameless Polydeukes.
She mingled in love with Kronion, lord of dark clouds,
5 under the peak of Taygetos, that lofty mountain,
and bore these children as saviors of men on this earth
and of swift-sailing ships, whenever wintry storms
sweep along the pitiless sea. Then men go
to the edge of the stern and with offers of white lambs
10 they pray and call upon the sons of great Zeus.
When great winds and the waves of the sea
bring the ship under water, they suddenly appear,
having sped through the air with rushing wings,

and forthwith they calm the cruel windy storms
15 and level the waves of the foaming high seas.
For the sailors' labor these are fair signs, and when they see them
they rejoice and quit their toilsome struggle.
Hail, Tyndaridai, riders of swift horses!
But I shall remember you and another song, too.

 TO GUEST-FRIENDS

Have respect for him who longs for your gifts and your houses,
all you who dwell in the lofty city of Hera, the lovely-faced nymph,
at the foot of towering Saidene,
drinking the divine water of the fair-flowing river,
5 the tawny Hermos, whom immortal Zeus sired.

Notes

1. TO DIONYSOS

We cannot be absolutely sure that these two fragments are part of the same hymn. The title *Eiraphiotes,* which occurs in both fragments, is a positive but hardly adequate indication. On the other hand, it is difficult to find one peremptory argument proving that our two fragments do not belong to the same hymn. The first nine lines are quoted by Diodorus Siculus (3.66.3). Lines 10–21 are found on folium 31 of codex M. The date of composition must be early (8th to 6th cc. B.C.). Diodorus attributed it to Homer, and this is some indication of an early date. Lines 10–21 are definitely the conclusion to a longer hymn. These lines are found in such a position in M—a whole quire and a leaf just before folium 31 are missing—that our fragment might well have belonged to a hymn that was 400-600 lines long.

1 Eiraphiotes: The ancients too puzzled over the meaning and etymology of this word. One of their explanations—and incidentally the one which prevailed in the minds of the ancients—connects the word with *rhaptô* (to sew) and alludes to the traditional version of the myth according to which Zeus rescued the yet unborn child from the ashes of his burnt mother and *sewed him into* his thigh. Modern explanations, including Sonne's, who draws a parallel with Sanskrit *ṛshabḥa* (bull), are more ingenious than convincing.

1 Drakanon: most likely a cape on the island of Cos.

2 Ikaros: island near Samos. Naxos: one of the Cycladic islands.

4 The traditional account gives Thebes as the birthplace of Dionysos and Semele as his mother; another mythological tradition makes him the offspring of an incestuous union between Zeus and his own daughter, Persephone.

8 Nysa: This is such a frequent toponym, found as far as India, that it would be unwise to be dogmatic about its precise location. The author of this hymn obviously accepts the theory that the name of the god is derived from the name of his father (*Zeus,* gen. *Dios*) and the name of his birthplace, which he places somewhere near Egypt.

11 Codex M contains an incomprehensible reading here. I have translated Allen's emendation for lack of something more convincing. That the dismemberment of Dionysos as Zagreus may be alluded to here is an attractive hypothesis. But since the Titans dismembered Dionysos, I fail to see why we should have "he cut (you)." The triennial festivals (*trietêrides*) of our line would be celebrated on alternate years according to our way of reckoning.

17 Whoever has read the *Bacchae* of Euripides would easily agree that *gynaimanês* ("woman-maddener") is a very apt epithet for Dionysos.

21 Here Thyône is another name for Semele. In some sources she is a nurse of Dionysos and in others she is given as his mother with no implication that this is an alternative name.

2. TO DEMETER

The earliest mention of Zeus' union with Demeter and of the rape of Persephone by Aidoneus is found in Hesiod's *Theogony* 912-14. The *Iliad* and the *Odyssey* ignore the story, but this is no proof that Homer did not know about it. It is possible that its purely chthonic character may have struck him as incongruous with the Olympic pantheon that dominates his epics. Of the subsequent treatments of the subject—and there were many—I should like to mention Euripides' *Helena* 1301–68, Kallimachos'*Hymn to Demeter* 6, and Ovid's *Fasti* 4, 419–616 and *Metamorphoses* 5. 385–661. The date of the hymn cannot be fixed with great precision. Both archeological evidence from the site of Eleusis and internal evidence from the hymn point to a date that cannot be later than the end of the seventh century. The "Hall of Rites" (*telestērion*), which must have been built when Eleusis came under Athenian control some time at the very end of the seventh century, is not mentioned in the hymn. This rather powerful argument establishes the end of the seventh century as a *terminus ante quem* for the composition of the hymn. The terrace structure, now referred to as *temenos*, seems to have been built in the eighth century. However, it is not this structure but rather the one described as Megaron B—situated on the east slope of the citadel of Eleusis—that must be the temple referred to in the *Hymn to Demeter* 270–74. It was discovered by Kourouniotes in the excavation of 1931 and 1932 and it dates from Mycenaean times (15th to 13th cc. B.C.). The *Marmor Parium* places the advent of Demeter to Eleusis in the fifteenth century. Greek tradition held that Eumolpos, the founder of the powerful sacerdotal order of the Eumolpids, was a contemporary of Erechtheus, who also belongs to the fifteenth century. Aristotle has preserved for us the tradition that the Eleusinia were instituted *c.* 1300 B.C. All this points to an early, Mycenaean origin of Demeter's cult at Eleusis. (For the identification of Megaron B with the temple of the hymn see George Mylonas, *Eleusis and the Eleusinian Mysteries*, Princeton, 1961, pp.33–49.) However, this evidence does not help us establish a *terminus post quem* for the composition of the hymn. It is certainly much later in time than the tradition that it preserves. More helpful in dating it is the absence of any reference to Athens. Since Eleusis came under Athenian control sometime in the second half of the seventh century, it may have been composed in the first half of the seventh century. The absence of any reference to Athens speaks not only for this earlier date but also for an Eleusinian rhapsode as the author.

The *Hymn to Demeter* is above all a poem of great beauty. But it has been studied more for what it can tell us about the Eleusinian mysteries and less for its poetic beauty. Since the initiates to the mysteries were sworn to secrecy with regard to the rituals that took place inside the *telestērion,* it is small wonder that we know next to nothing about those rituals. The telltale accounts of early Christian zealots are not worthless, but we must not forget that they are biased polemics. Yet, the hymn yields valuable information not only about the preparation for initiation and the significance of the ritualistic regimen but also about the very nature of Demeter's cult at Eleusis. Thus the hymn leaves no doubt that whatever went on at Eleusis dealt with the mystery of life and regeneration as well as with the impenetrable secret of death and the hope for some ray of light in the tenebrous underworld. Furthermore, the hymn teaches us that the cult was chthonic, most likely pre-Hellenic in origin and indigenous to Eleusis. By this I do not mean that similar cults did not exist elsewhere. Far from it. I only mean that the Eleusinian version of what is in essence a human universal and a religious archetype had its own distinct identity, which need not have been imported from somewhere else. As Jane Harrison aptly put it, "Demeter at Eleusis did not borrow her cymbals from Rhea, she had her own." (*Prolegomena to the Study of Greek Religion,* 4th printing, 3d ed., New York, 1960, p. 561.)

3   "Gave" is both appropriate and consistent with Zeus' position as "father of gods and men." Of course, "gave" here almost means permitted or allowed, but the notion of giving Persephone away as a bride is also inherent. Hesiod expresses the same idea in *Theogony* 914. Later versions of the story, which make Zeus act under the constraint of Moira or have Pluto fall victim to the designs of a capricious Venus, must be the result of learned mythographic speculation or of poetic fancy.

4   Scholars have not been able to determine the propriety or significance of the adjective that I am translating "of the golden sword." Lycophron mentions an obscure cult of the sword-bearing Demeter in Boeotia and it is possible that this cult was a survival from an earlier, more widespread aspect of the cult of Demeter.

5–14   The presence of the Okeanidai cannot be of any special significance. It may simply enhance the atmosphere of maidenly innocence. However, the gathering of flowers is not mere poetic embellishment and must correspond to ritualistic aspects of the worship of Demeter and Persephone as goddesses of vegetation. Survivals of flower-gathering festivals can still be found in most rural communities of Greece. It is interesting that, although other flowers are present in the poem, the narcissus is given the prominence that it doubtless deserved as a flower especially connected with the Great Goddesses (cf. Sophocles, *Oedipus Coloneus* 683). The chthonic nature of this flower is evident in its being sacred to the Eumenides, and Artemidoros tells us that it was also funereal (*Oneirokritikos* 1.77). The association of the narcissus with death could be attributed both to its real or presumed soporific qualities and to the fact that in myth it was the lure that led to the rape of Persephone and her sojourn in Hades for one third of the year during which nature "died."

17   Scholarly efforts to identify the Nysian field have not yielded any credible results.

23   We should not be surprised that a Mediterranean poet chose to endow the olive trees with the ability to hear. The Greeks, ancient and modern, frequently grant human attributes not only to animals but also to inanimate objects. One of the earliest instances is to be found in *Iliad* 3.275–80. In the song of *Constantine and Arete* birds speak, and a Cretan singer from the days of the Second World War begins his song with the line: "What ails the mountains of Crete, and they stand about with tearful eyes?"

24   This is one of the earliest references to Hekate, who is the daughter of the Titan Persês (so spelled in other sources) and Asteriê (cf. Hesiod *Theogony* 411). The fact that she is not mentioned in Homer testifies not only to a relatively late arrival in Greece, most likely from the East, but also to a date of composition later than that of the two great Homeric epics.

42   It is odd that Demeter wears a dark veil, a sign of mourning, even before she hears of her daughter's abduction. We may be faced with a case in which later ritual influences mythopoetic composition.

47   The number of days may indeed be conventional. But, although we do not know the exact duration of the fast, either at the Eleusinian mysteries or at the *Thesmophoria,* we do know that the period of strict mourning after someone's death as well as certain expiatory rites lasted for nine days. The number three and its multiples were frequently employed then as even now. Thus, the Graces were three, the Muses nine, the Olympian gods twelve, etc. When Apollon attacks the Achaean camp with his pestiferous arrows, he does so for nine whole days (*Iliad* 1.53). Dêô, most likely a diminutive, is another name for Demeter.

48   In the myth Demeter holds torches in her hands because she is searching—one presumes—especially dark caves and wooded glens in which the abductor might have sought refuge. In the ritual of the Eleusinian mysteries and the *Thesmophoria,* the torches may have been symbols of the solar light and warmth that must triumph over the infernal cold and darkness of the winter so that nature may come alive again in the spring.

49-50   These tokens of extreme grief are not substantially different from those practiced by the Greeks of today during the Holy Week and especially on Good Friday. Devout Christians follow a certain dietary regimen during the Holy Week and abstain from all festive activities. On the Saturday preceding Easter Sunday, and usually at midnight, there is a light-giving ceremony and, after the conclusion of the liturgy, participants carry the light of the Resurrection to their homes. (cf. *Iliad* 23.43-48).

52   The author of this hymn definitely identifies Hekate with the moon, and the torch must be symbolic of the lunar light emanating from Hekate, the moon-goddess.

62   The sun does see everything and so he watches gods and men. Similarly, the moon sees all and it is no accident that the cry of Persephone did not escape either Helios or Hecate. The idea of the all-seeing sun is commonplace in Greek poetry down to the present day. Thus Homer's "O sun, you who see and hear all things" (*Iliad* 3.277) is reechoed by Kazantzakis in "Great sun, who pass on high yet watch all things below" (*The Odyssey, a Modern Sequel, Prol.* 17).

74   Hyperionidês (the son of Hyperion) is a patronymic; the usual form is Hyperiôn as in *Odyssey* 1.8 (cf. also *Hymn to Apollon* 369).

96   Keleos, his wife Metaneira, and even his daughters were still revered at Eleusis in classical times (cf. Paus. 1.39 and Clement of Alexandria 1.39).

99   The Parthenion has not been convincingly identified with any modern landmark. In ancient times it came to be confused with another well, the Kallichoron, which was near the precinct of Eleusis.

101   Disguises in order to conceal true identity are in keeping with the conventions of the Greek epic. Aphrodite appears to Helen in the guise of an old woman (*Iliad* 3.386-89) and to Anchises as a young Phrygian maiden (Hymn to Aphrodite 81-83, 107-42).

109-10   Pausanias, on the authority of Homer (?) and Pamphos, names only three daughters and gives them names other than the ones in the text of the hymn (1.38.3).

75

122 Dôs is not an unlikely pseudonym for Demeter. The word occurs as a substantive in Hesiod *Works and Days* 356 and is equivalent to *dosis* (giving). The goddess is playful because on the one hand she does not give her true name but on the other hand her pseudonym begins with the same letter and has a meaning that is highly suggestive of Demeter's nature as a generous and "giving" divinity.

123 Some have tried to discover the origin of the Eleusinian cult in this story. But the story of a young girl kidnapped by Cretan pirates may be no more than a convenient lie. Odysseus pretends that he is a Cretan on three different occasions (*Odyssey* 13.256; 14.199; 19.172).

126 Thorikos was north of Cape Sounion.

153 In classical times Triptolemos became a very important figure in the Eleusinian mysteries. Here he is merely another one of the local princes, a fact which testifies to the great antiquity of the hymn. His parentage is uncertain, but for Apollodoros he is the eldest son of Keleos and Metaneira (1.5.2). Dioklos may be the same as the Megarian hero Dioklês and his inclusion here may not be unrelated to the dependence of Eleusis on Megara in earlier times.

154-55 Although some later sources make Dolichos the son of Triptolemos, Polyxeinos, Eumolpos and Dolichos are otherwise unknown.

188-89 Demeter's head touches the roof much as Aphrodite's does in the *Hymn to Aphrodite* 173-174. The Greeks generally ascribed superhuman stature to the gods (cf. *Iliad* 4.443). Radiance as a token of divine presence (cf. *Hymn to Apollon* 444) has found ready acceptance in Christian accounts of miraculous epiphany.

191-205 This charming and intriguing incident in the story of Demeter's search for Persephone is still awaiting the day on which some incisive mind will shed light on its origins and implications. On the surface the story is simple: Demeter is deeply distraught and a funny old lady tells her some coarse, most likely mimetic jokes, and makes her smile and laugh. But who is Iambê, and why in the Orphic version is it not Iambê but the Eleusinian queen, Baubô, who induces the goddess to forget her sorrow and laugh by lifting her robe and exposing her pudenda? From ancient sources we know that at nearly every festival in honor of Demeter, including the procession to Eleusis (cf. Aristophanes *Frogs* 372ff.), there was frivolity in the form of obscene gestures and jesting. We have reason to believe that the gestures and jests were sexual in character and, thus, a most appropriate part of a fertility cult. For the Orphic version of the story see *Orphicorum Fragmenta* 46-53 (Kern)—especially fragment 52—and Clement of Alexandria in *Protreptikos* 2.20,1-21,2.

207-8 It should be mentioned here that most sacrifices to Demeter and to many other chthonic gods were wineless. The reason for this taboo remains unknown.

208-10 The Greek word for this potion is *kykeôn* (literally, a mixed or stirred drink). On the authority of Clement of Alexandria we know that a mixture of water, mint (pennyroyal), and meal was used as a drink of initiation into the Eleusinian mysteries. However, this act of initiation must not have been part of the secret and ineffable rites performed at the *telestêrion* (Hall of Rituals), because depictions of it are found on Attic vases.

228-30 In "the Undercutter" and "the tree-felling creature" scholars have, I think rightly, seen references to the belief that toothache is caused by a certain worm. The goddess wisely refers to it with a periphrasis for fear that calling it by its name might provoke its instant appearance.

1–41 Parallels to the story of Demophoôn are found not only in Greek literature but also in the legends of other nations (cf. the story of Isis and the infant son of the king of Byblos in Plutarch's *Isis and Osiris* 16). In Greek literature the story of Thetis and Achilles shows that the motif is not confined to this hymn. Apollodoros and other later writers depart from the tradition of this hymn and, accommodating the eventual prominence of Triptolemos in the Eleusinian mysteries, tell us either that Demophoôn died when Demeter's strange doings were discovered by Metaneira (Apollodoros 1.5.1) or that the child nursed by Demeter was not Demophoôn but Triptolemos (cf. among others Ovid *Metamorphoses* 5.645; Nicander *Thêriaka* 484). As Demeter herself explains in lines 260–61 the purpose of anointing Demophoôn with ambrosia and hiding him in the fire by night was to make him immortal. The reader may recall that Thetis put drops of ambrosia into the nose of Patroklos to prevent decay of his skin (*Iliad* 19.39). According to Lycophron (*Cassandra* 178ff.), Thetis immortalized six of her children by burning away their mortal parts in the fire. Her attempt to make Achilles immortal by placing him on the fire and then by anointing him with ambrosia was frustrated by Peleus, who intervened just when the goddess had subjected all but the ankle-bone of the child to this treatment (Apollodoros 3.13.6). It is interesting that fire and ambrosia are used both in the case of Achilles and Demophoôn. As Apollodoros tells the story, Thetis hid Achilles in the fire by night and anointed him with ambrosia by day. Although in the story of Demophoôn it is not clear what procedure is followed, the treatment with fire took place at night, the implication thereby being that the anointing occurred during the day. Perhaps the origin of using fire and then ambrosia to make someone immortal may not be unconnected with the smith's technique, who first "hides" the metal in fire and then dips it in water to harden it.

65–67 We know of no civil war at Eleusis and this may indeed be an *ex post facto* prophecy, in which case, given the antiquity of the hymn, we may be dealing with a facet of Eleusinian history antedating the prominence that Eleusis gained as a result of the cult of Demeter.

70–72 For the identification of the temple mentioned in these lines see G. E. Mylonas, *Eleusis and the Eleusinian Mysteries,* 34ff. The *Kallichoron* was discovered in 1892.

292 Keleos, the child's father, knows nothing as yet. This nocturnal propitiation of the goddess is solely attended by women and may correspond to the *pannychis,* the all-night women's festival, of the *Thesmophoria.*

302 *Xanthos* ("blond") must be used as conventionally here as elsewhere in Greek epic (cf. 279).

305–13 It has not been determined whether these lines conceal a reference to lean years of famine and destitution for the Eleusinians, destitution that the Eleusinians were known to have once suffered.

349 Erebos here means "darkness."

358 "Smiling brows," the literal translation of the expression, is at first sight a strange expression. Modern Greeks use the expression "even his moustache laughed" and signal

"no" by swiftly raising their eyebrows. Thus, "smiling brows" may be a reference to an especially Greek facial expression or merely a hyperbole for "he really smiled."

372–74   Apollodoros follows the hymn closely with respect to line 372 (cf. 1.5.3). In Ovid's *Metamorphoses* 5.535, Persephone is not given the fruit by the god of the Underworld, but she finds it in a garden and eats seven seeds. Some obscure numerological allusion may be hidden in this version. The pomegranate was widely used both in ritual and folk medicine, but our poet may have chosen it rather than some other fruit because the plant had definite chthonic connections. The tree was thought to have sprung from the blood of Dionysos Zagreus (Clement of Alexandria, *Protreptikos,* 2.19) and pomegranate seeds are still used by Greeks as decorations in the *kollyba,* wheat offerings that are distributed to the congregation in memorial services in honor of the dead. By eating of a fruit that is especially connected with the world of the dead and by accepting what is a gift from the ruler of that world, Persephone establishes a *xenia,* a guest-host tie that comes with an obligation for her both to come back and to give in return.

390–93   For a variation on this version, cf. Ovid *Metamorphoses* 5.534.

399   Of the explanations given for Persephone's sojourn in Hades for one third of the year the ancient Stoic doctrine that this period stood for the time during which seeds are "hidden" in the ground is certainly both logical and plausible. One might add that the Greek winter lasts for about one third of the year. However the reader should know that most of the text of lines 387–400 has been restored and that, therefore, everything pertaining to these lines is highly conjectural.

438–40   For Hekate, cf. Hesiod *Theogony* 411ff. The association of Hekate with Demeter and Persephone is understandable. She is frequently confused with Artemis and closely associated with Selene, the Moon, whose role in women's menstrual cycle is too obvious to need elaboration.

450   Rharion has not been identified with a definite place in the vicinity of Eleusis, where Stephanus Byzantinus places it.

460   Demeter is the daughter of Kronos and Rhea.

476   The Greek word for which I translate "celebration" is *drêsmosynê* (enactment); thus the emphasis is definitely on a sacred *drama* in which the story of Demeter and Persephone was acted out by priests of the cult.

479   The *hierokêryx* (literally "sacred herald") proclaimed silence with the word *euphêmeite,* "keep reverent silence", and the initiates complied. The injunction not to divulge the sacred rites must rather refer to the sworn secrecy that was imposed upon the initiates. The reasons for this secrecy are not immediately obvious. Secret religious or semireligious societies still swear their members to secrecy on certain aspects of their initiations and their practices, and followers of transcendental meditation are not supposed to reveal their *mantra* to others. Some have supposed that the *drômena*—which we may translate the "acting rites"—of the Eleusinian mysteries were kept secret because their revelation would rob them of their power. Others have seen in these mysteries an ancient chthonic cult of the original inhabitants of Eleusis, who were anxious to keep it secret from their Indo-European conquerors. I think that secrecy was imposed in order to protect the rites

from vulgarization and frivolous mimicry and to keep them as the private preserve, as it were, of the few families from which the priests of this prestigious cult were drawn.

0–82 For the sentiment, cf. Aristophanes *Frogs* 455–59; Pindar fr. 137; Plato *Phaedrus* 69c; Euripides *Heracles* 613ff., et al. The bliss of the initiates may have stemmed from their communion with divinities connected with the whole cycle of life from birth to death and from their participation in holy rites that revealed to them that death was only part of this cycle and not the end of it.

489 In Orphic Hymn 40.3, Demeter is described as *ploutodoteira,* "giver of wealth" (*ploutos* means "wealth" in Greek) and in the *Thesmophoriazousai* of Aristophanes (296), *Ploutos* is invoked in prayer after Demeter and Persephone. In art *Ploutos* is often represented as a boy with cornucopia or corn-basket. One may conjecture that in addition to psychic bliss and hope for afterlife, the initiates were also promised material wealth as a reward for their sharing in the sacred rites.

491 The cult of Demeter at Paros is well-known both from inscriptions and other evidence. The scholiast on the *Birds* of Aristophanes, line 1764, informs us that Archilochos had composed a hymn to Parian Demeter. *Antron* was a Thessalian town mentioned in the *Iliad* 2.697.

3. TO APOLLON

The Homeric *Hymn to Apollon* has come down to us as the second longest and the oldest of the thirty-three Homeric Hymns. We have both the name of the author and the date of composition on the authority of the Sicilian chronicler Hippostratos (3d c. B.C.). Hippostratos tells us that the author was a certain Kynaithos from the island of Chios, "who first recited the poems of Homer at Syracuse in the sixty-ninth Olympiad." Scholars find no objection to the name of the poet, but they consider the date given (504 B.C.) as far too late to explain certain glaring omissions in the poem. The most prominent among these are the Pythia, the splendid Pythian games, which became Panhellenic, the chasm, the burning of the first Delphic temple, and the building of the temple to Apollo on the island of Delos. The hymn must antedate the burning of the Delphic temple in 548 B.C. (for this temple, which was built by Trophonios and Agamedes, see lines 294–99). But the rhapsode Kynaithos may have recited from the Homeric epics in Syracuse shortly after the foundation of that city in 733 B.C. He may also have composed the *Hymn to Apollon* earlier, perhaps, in the middle of the eighth century B.C. If this not unreasonable conjecture be true, our poet was a contemporary of Hesiod and of Eumelos of Corinth. In keeping with rhapsodic practice, Kynaithos must have composed the hymn as a *prooimion,* a prelude that is, to the recitation of longer portions from the Homeric epics. It is perhaps due to this fact that confusion arose as to the authorship of the preludes. They were Homeric in style and they preceded the recitation of truly Homeric pieces by rhapsodes, who frequently referred to themselves as Homeridai, sons of Homer.

The fact that a portion of the hymn is dedicated to the Delian Apollon and another longer portion to the Delphic Apollon has led some scholars to propound the theory that we are dealing with two poems by two different authors or, at least, with two poems by the same author. The separatists consider line 178 the last line of one hymn and line 179 the beginning of another. Internal evidence from the poem has been marshaled forth to support this theory, and a misunderstood passage from Thucydides (3.104) has added to the confusion. What the separatists have failed to understand is that the poet of the hymn was not a professor of history or archeology, but a bard schooled in the digressive, leisurely, and frequently omissive manner of the epic tradition. He composed his poem in order to please and entertain pilgrims and festive celebrants, rather than to satisfy the demands of carping literary critics and of poetic surgeons. This is not to say that the poet of the hymn does not teach us much about history, archeology and religion. Quite the contrary. But he also teaches us much about Apollon as the Greeks imagined him and felt his divine power. Today's approach, subject as it is to the brutal dictates of a faithless age, will not concede that Apollon changed into a dolphin or that he slew the dragon at Delphi. A Greek peasant, whose gods and saints still perform such miracles, will have no trouble believing the poet. Thus, the poet of our hymn can communicate with much less trouble with the Greek peasant than with the learned specialist. The visitor—or rather the pilgrim—who goes to Delos or Delphi will do well to lend the poet a gentle and reverent ear, because the poet tells the truth, the religious and poetic truth, than which none is higher even in these god-forsaken times.

1–4   The poet introduces Apollon as the archer par excellence. When he strings his bow the gods are startled. For a far more elaborate passage on stringing a bow, cf. *Odyssey* 21. 409ff. Leto, the mother of Apollon and Artemis, was a Titaness and daughter of Phoibe and Koios (Hesiod *Theogony* 404–10). Not many Titans were worshiped in historical times, but Leto was frequently worshiped either together with her two children or separately (e.g., on Delos and Phaistos, where there was a Lêtôon, a temple dedicated to Leto).

14–18   In these lines the poet tips his hat, as it were, to Apollon's mother, as it is quite proper to show respect to Leto, who is not only the mother of Apollon but also a goddess herself. It is interesting that the poet of our hymn has her seated among the Olympians. This is more due to his imagination and his desire to elevate her position than to any traditional inclusion of Leto in the Olympian pantheon. Both Homer and Hesiod know that Leto is the mother of Apollon and Artemis (cf. Homer *Iliad* 1.9 and 36; 16.849; 24.605ff; and Hesiod *Theogony* 918–20), but they do not give us an account of the circumstances of their births. Some have identified *Ortygiê* (16) with the Syracusan Ortygia. The Greek geographer Strabo identified it with Rheneia (cf. *Odyssey* 15.403–4). It should be mentioned here that other places besides Delos, such as Lycia and Ephesos, claimed to have been Apollon's birthplace. Leto leaned against the hill (Kynthos, 17) and thus clearly was imagined to have borne the god at the foot of this granite hill near the famous and well-attested palm tree and the mostly dry stream of the Inopos (18), which has been identified in modern times by Ross. It is interesting that on the top of Kynthos, Zeus, Apollon, and Artemis shared both a cult and the epithet Kynthios, and that the *Diana Cynthia* of later times was thought to have been born together with Apollon on Delos.

22 It has been conjectured, and with good reason, that the Christianized Greeks have so frequently built temples to St. Elias on mountain peaks and hilltops, because the partial homonymy between his name and that of Apollon Helios (Sun) furnished them with an occasion to retain an old, deeply rooted cult under an acceptable name.

27–28 The wave was a portent attending the miraculous birth.

30–44 These lines read like a pilgrim's guide to Apollon's shrines. But, although most of the places mentioned did have Apollonian cults, the manner in which the places are given draws more attention to the extent of Leto's wanderings. According to legend the Athenian hero Theseus founded the Delian festival in honor of Apollon on his return to Athens from Crete. There were many places named Aigai in ancient Greece. The one mentioned in line 32 may be an island near Euboea (cf. Hesychios s.v.). The identification of Eiresiai (32) with Pliny's Irrhesia on the Thermaic gulf (*Natural History* 4.72) is very doubtful. Peparêthos (32) is next to Skiathos in the northwest Aegean (now on the map as Skopelos). Thracian Samos (34) is surely Samothrace in the north Aegean and Ida, of course, is not the Cretan Ida, but Homer's Trojan Ida. Phôkaia (35) was on the coast of Asia Minor, southeast of Lesbos, and Autokanê may have been situated also on the coast of Asia Minor opposite the south point of Lesbos. Imbros and Lêmnos are on the northwest corner of the Aegean and easy to find on the map, although on non-Greek maps Imbros may now bear the name given it by its Turkish masters. Makar (37), usually known as Makareus, was discovered by his father, Aiolos, to have incestuous relations with his sister (Ovid *Heroides* 11; Hyginus *Fabula* 242). For Makar as ruler and law-giver on Lesbos see Diodorus Siculus 5.82. Mimas (39) was in the Erythraean peninsula and opposite Chios, and Kôrykos (39) was the south promontory of the same peninsula. Klaros (40), located near the city of Kolophôn on the coast of Asia Minor (near modern Tsille), had both an oracle and a temple dedicated to Apollon. Aisageê (40) has not been identified. Mt. Mykalê (41) was opposite Samos on the coast of Asia Minor. Those who are curious about the relationship of *Meropes* (42) to *meropes* (mortal) in the Greek epic might wish to read H. Koller's excellent article in *Glotta*, 46, 1968, 18ff. Both Knidos and Karpathos (43) had Apollonian cults. Rhênaia (44), usually spelt Rhêne(i)a, is the much larger island west of Delos.

47 The places that Leto visited refused to be Apollon's birthplace because they feared the angry jealousy of Hera. Pausanias tells us that, according to Tegean legend, the reluctant offenders were later punished by Apollon and Artemis (8.53.1). In another version of the same story, Leto traveled in the form of a she-wolf from the land of the Hyperboreans to Delos in twelve days (Aristotle *H.A.* 580A, Aelian *N.A.* 4.4 and 11.1). The bronze statue of a she-wolf shown at Delphi in ancient times was doubtless connected with this story.

58 Hecatombs, originally sacrifices of a hundred oxen, were especially connected with the

worship of Apollon, and Ionian communities named a month *Hekatombaiôn* after the festival of Apollon Hekatombaios.

64–65 In this reference to the unpleasant sound of Delos, the poet is most likely giving us his version of the etymology of the name of the island by implying a derivation from the root *dêl*—seen in *dêleomai* (to harm) and *dêlëeis* (baneful). The most probable view, and one held by some of the ancients, is that Delos means "clear, conspicuous."

73–75 The idea that Delos was a floating island up to the birth of Apollon is later, and these lines do not contain a hidden reference to what must have been a product of poetic fancy.

79–82 The oracle on Delos, attested by a single inscription (*IG* XI.2.165V.44), must have sunk into insignificance and obscurity so early that our classical sources are virtually silent on it.

84–86 For the solemnity of the oath, cf. *Iliad* 15.36–37. The Styx is invoked as a dread representative of Underworld powers, which sanction the oath and may also visit the perjurer with punishment.

92–96 Most of the goddesses named in these lines are among the Titans (cf. Hesiod *Theogony* 135 and Apollodoros 1.1.3). The phrase "other immortal goddesses" of line 95 is rather vague, and we cannot but notice the chthonic character of the attending divinities. The title Ichnaian for Themis (94) had few cults, but she was present at the birth of Athena (Paus. 3.17.3) and of Aphrodite (Paus. 5.11.8).

97 Eileithyia is the divine midwife and daughter of Zeus and Hera (Hesiod *Theogony* 922). In Homer she is controlled by Hera, who delays the birth of Herakles by preventing Eileithyia from attending (*Iliad* 19.119). In historical times Eileithyia was worshipped not only on Delos but also throughout the Cyclades, Crete, and the mainland.

102 Iris is regularly used as divine messenger (cf. *Hymn to Demeter,* 314).

107 Cf. *Iliad* 5.368.

114 Cf. *Iliad* 5.778; Arist. *Birds* 575.

117 The palm tree of the holy precinct of Apollon is mentioned in *Odyssey* 6.162 and was reported as still alive in the days of Cicero (*Laws* 1.1) and of Pliny (*Natural History* 16.89).

117–18 Statues of kneeling women about to give birth and of goddesses of birth do suggest that this position was commonly assumed by laboring women in ancient Greece.

124 In the *Hymn to Demeter* (2.237) Demeter anoints Demophoôn with ambrosia in order to make him immortal. Aristaios is made immortal by feeding on nectar and ambrosia (Pindar *Pythian Ode* 9.63).

127–29 For the precocity of the divine babe, cf. *Hymn to Hermes* 15–19.

136–38 These lines are found only in some of the manuscripts.

146–57 By the end of the fifth century B.C. the Ionians no longer flocked to Delos for this great festival, but instead gathered at Ephesos on the Asiatic coast. Thucydides reports that adversities, which he does not specify, were responsible for the waning of this splendid festival (see Thuc. 3.104). We may conjecture that, as the Delphic festival grew in importance, the Delian festival must have slowly declined in inverse proportion.

The Delian chorus took part in other festivals and also performed on the occasion of sacred embassies to the sanctuary.

57–64 The Delian Maidens obviously followed a certain hierarchic order in their performance. They started with a hymn to Apollon, Artemis, and Leto, the divine mother; then they sang a song in praise of heroes. Finally, in what must have been mimetic sketches in the various dialects of the pilgrims, they provided them with light-hearted entertainment. The sequence was thus in descending order (gods-heroes-men), and in typical Greek fashion the solemnity of the festival was tempered with a note of frivolity at the end.

65–78 In these lines the poet asks the Delian maidens to make him the poet laureate, as it were, of the Delian festival. In exchange he promises to make their skill in song known far and wide and never to "cease to hymn far-shooting Apollon." Given the conventions of early Greek epic poetry, the directness of the poet is remarkable. There is no doubt that contests were held during the Delian festival. The Hesiodic fragment 265 teaches us this much:

"First then Homer and I as singers composed song
in youthful hymns in which we sang
of Phoibos Apollon of the golden sword whom Leto bore."

Lines 171–73 must have originated the tradition that Homer was a blind poet from Chios. Combining lines 165–78 with the above fragment 265 one might for a moment imagine that if the blind poet of our hymn were Homer, Hesiod might well be his competitor, but unfortunately this enticing conjecture would meet with a wall of formidable objections.

79–80 These are Apollon's Asiatic haunts and as such most welcome to those who hold the view that Apollon came to Greece from Asia. Some scholars have connected Lykia (Lycia) with the cult epithet *lyk(e)ios* and *Lykêgenês* (*Iliad* 4.101). But opinions are divided on *lyk(e)ios* and *Lykêgenês*. Some scholars think that these words basically stem from the toponym Lykiê. Others, depending on their views about the origin of Apollon, connect their root with that of Latin *lux* (light). This is a sufficiently attractive derivation, but it does not satisfy those who see the Greek word *lykos* (wolf) as a more probable linguistic kinsman of the disputed epithets. Patara, where the god was thought to spend six months of the year, was in Lydia, while Karia (Caria) boasted of a famous Apollonian oracle at Didyma (Branchidae) to the south of Miletos. Further north were the famous oracle and temple at Klaros (Ionia) and a similar combination of shrine and oracle at Gryneion (Aeolia).

88–89 Cf. Hesiod *Shield* 201 and Pindar *Nemean Ode* 5.22.

194 The Graces (Charites) and the Seasons (Horae) are most frequently associated with Aphrodite (cf. *Iliad* 5.338; *Odyssey* 18. 194; *Cypria* 5). The haunts of the Graces are near those of the Muses on Olympos (Hesiod *Theogony* 64) and they are associated with Apollon in literature (Pindar *Olympian Ode* 14.10) and in art (Paus. 9.35.1). Plutarch (*Moralia* 1136A) tells us that on Delos there was a statue of Apollon with the bow in his right hand and the three Graces in his left. The cult epithet *hôromedôn* (*IG* XII.5.893), roughly translated "ruler of the Seasons," as well as similar epithets also show a close connection of Apollon with the seasons. The Hesiodic Horae (*Theogony* 900–903) are daughters of Zeus and Themis and their names (Eunomia, Dikê, Eirenê) point more to

their legal and pacific character. However, in general, they were kindly divinities associated with the changes of the seasons and the growth of vegetation. Their first representation is on the François vase and their concept has been beautifully treated in neoclassical art (Thorvaldsen) and music (Vivaldi).

195   Harmonia was the daughter of Ares and Aphrodite. She was given to Kadmos as his wife and gave birth to the ill-fated Agave. Her necklace played an important role in the Theban saga. Hebe was the daughter of Zeus and Hera. She was also cup-bearer to the gods (*Iliad* 4.2) and was given to Heracles as his wife (*Odyssey* 11.603). In cult she was quite unimportant.

196   Cf. the beautiful dance scene in *Iliad* 18.590–94.

197   Cf. *Odyssey* 6.101–7.

208–13   The daughter of Azan may be Koronis (she is usually the daughter of the Lapith Phlegyas). We do know that Ischys, son of Elatos, was a rival of Apollon (Hesiod fr. 125; Pindar *Pythian Ode* 3.55). Phorbas and Ereutheus may have been Apollon's rivals for the love of Koronis, but the text is such that the presence of each rival may imply a fresh object of contention. Leukippos (212) courted Daphne and approached her in the guise of a woman. This however did not deceive Daphne and her companions, who killed him when they discovered his sex (Paus. 8.20.3).

216   Apollon had been received on Olympos (186) before he started his search for the site of his oracle. Pierie is north of Olympos.

217   Lektos may have been a harbor or a coastal town. The Ainianes lived at the springs of the Spercheios.

218–21   The Perrhaiboi lived round Larissa in Thessaly. From Iolkos near the Pagasitic gulf he came to cape Kênaion at the extreme northwest tip of Euboea. His next stop, the Lelantine plain, is to be found between Chalkis and Eretria.

222–24   The mountain must be Messapios across from Chalkis. Mykalessos is beyond Aulis and southeast of it at the foot of Mt. Messapios. Teumessos is the modern Mesovouvi, a small village about five miles from Thebes.

225–28   The abode of Thebe is of course the city of Thebes. Thebe was daughter of the river god Asopos and twin sister of Aigina. She became the bride of Zethos and gave her name to the city that was previously known as Kadmeia. Apollon's cult in Thebes must have flourished at times.

230–38   Both the grove and the temple were famous in antiquity (*Iliad* 2.506; Hesiod fr. 219; Alcaeus fr. Z102 LP (7 Loeb); Pindar *Isthmian Ode* 1.33, and others). Pausanias reports that when he visited the place, the town and the temple were in ruins, but the statue of Poseidon was still standing (9.26.3). The exact character and significance of the custom described in these lines are not clear. Of the many explanations offered so far those that consider the custom a specific rite performed on a certain occasion must be closer to the truth. The rider of the chariot leaps off and allows the horse or horses to race through the trees. If the chariot is not dashed against the trees, the god does not claim it as his. But if the chariot is broken, the rider interprets this as an indication of Poseidon's will to keep it.

)–43 The Kephissos (not to be confused with the better known Attic stream) flowed across the northern part of Lake Kopais. Okalea was near Lake Kopais, and Haliartos lay between Onchestos and Okalea. In view of the location of these places, the god's itinerary is not very logical. The travels of Leto (30–45) are beset with similar problems, which stem at times from metrical necessity and at other times from a poet's approach, which cannot be the same as that of a geographer.

244 This may be the same as the Tilphousa of Pausanias (9.33.1).

250 Peloponnesos is found here for the first time as a single word. It otherwise occurs as *Pelopos nêsos* (island of Pelops).

251 By Europe here the poet seems to mean northern Greece. Since Hesiod applies the name to a nymph (*Theogony* 357), this is surely the oldest application of the name to a geographical area.

44ff. According to our poet, no temple was built at Telphousa. Thus it may be futile to seek the remnants of such a temple at whichever place we identify as Telphousa.

272 Iêpaiêôn here is a cult epithet for Apollon. In lines 500 and 517 it is the name of the song sung in honor of the god. The popular ancient etymology of the word from *iê Paian* may not be incorrect simply because it was not advanced by modern linguists.

8–80 The Phlegyes were a tribe hostile to the Delphic precinct. Lake Kephisis is otherwise known as Kopais (Paus. 9.24.1; 9.36.2; 10.7.1).

1–99 On Delphi and the temple the reader is advised to consult Paus. 10.5.5ff.; Strabo 9.3; Courby *Fouilles de Delphes* 2.92. This is not the place for a history of the fortunes of the holy precinct, but it should be mentioned that the original temple was destroyed by fire or arson in 548 B.C., and that some years later, by 505 B.C., the Alcmeonids, aided by generous contributions by Amasis, Croesus, and other wealthy barbarians and Greeks, erected a splendid temple of Parian marble. For the legendary builders Trophonios and Agamedes (296) see Paus. 9.37.4 and [Plato] *Axiochos* 367c. Kris(s)a a few kilometers down from the Delphic hill attempted to control Delphi, but was destroyed at the end of the First Sacred War (585 B.C.).

300 We cannot be absolutely sure about the identification of this spring, but the Castalian spring seems a reasonable conjecture.

306 For Typhaôn (Typhoeus in 367) see Hesiod *Theogony* 306ff., 820ff.

3–36, For invoking chthonic deities or ghosts by striking the earth with the flat of the hand, cf. *Iliad* 9.568; Euripides *Troiades* 1306. For the origin and ancient etymology of the Titans (Titênes) see Hesiod *Theogony* 207–10. For the battle of the gods against the Titans see Hesiod *Theogony* 617ff. The common ancestry of gods and men is also mentioned in Hesiod *Works and Days* 108.

0–43 The earth was invoked along with the sky in line 334 in a manner reminiscent of similar invocations in modern Greek folk songs. Thus in the song that is sung in Cyprus, as the wheat used for the *resin,* the wedding meal of cracked wheat, is taken from the spring to the home of the bride or groom, the legendary young swain swears by the earth, the sky, the stars, and the moon. Now in 340–43 Hera strikes the earth, and the earth moves in order to show that Hera's wish will be granted. The earth is not an anthropomorphic goddess but a palpable elemental power, which is capable of hearing and responding.

352 Typhaôn and Typhoeus seem to be a generic name for monstrous creatures. The dread Typhaôn of Hesiod's *Theogony* 820ff. was a child of Earth (Gaia) and Tartaros.

367 Chimaira was the daughter of Typhaôn and Echidna (Hesiod *Theogony* 306, 319).

370–74 Of all the folk etymologies that the ancients gave in explanation of the origin of Pythô and Pytheios, this is the oldest and the best (cf. Paus. 10.6.5).

391–403 The story of the first Delphic priests' coming from Knossos and of Apollon's metamorphosis into a dolphin (Gr. *delphis*) certainly shows that our poet thought that the cult of Apollon Delphinios had strong ties with Crete. There was a temple of Apollon Delphinios at Knossos (*CIG* II.2554, Γ98), and the title *delphidios* was applied to Apollon in votive Cretan inscriptions on the island of Delos (*BCH* 3.293, 4.355). I also think that the poet of the hymn must have thought that the toponym Delphi stemmed from the fact that Apollon appeared to his priests in the shape of a dolphin.

396 This line has made some scholars think that the Delphic oracle was a tree oracle in the beginning. The reader will recall that the Selloi of Dodona practiced divination by interpreting the rustling of the leaves of the sacred oak. This is an attractive conjecture, but we need more evidence to support it. We do know that the first Delphic temple was built of laurel, that the priestess chewed leaves of laurel before she uttered her prophetic words, and that she also smoked herself with burning laurel before she descended into the cavern.

409–13 Maleia and Tainaron both were cities situated on the homonymous promontories of the southern Peloponnese.

422–24 For Arênê, birthplace of the Argonauts Lynkeus and Idas, cf. *Iliad* 2.591 and 11.723; also Apollonios Rhodios 1.152. Line 423 is identical with *Iliad* 2.592. Thryon and Aipy are discussed by Strabo 8.3.24ff. The Pylos of line 424 is the Triphylian one also discussed by Strabo (8.3.7ff.). Argyphea has not been identified.

425–26 Both Krounoi and Chalkis were small streams (cf. Strabo 8.3.13, 26ff.) in the district of Makistia to the south of the mouth of the Alpheios. Dymê, to the west of the mouth of the Peiros river and not very far from Patrai, is out of place in this catalogue. Homer also calls the inhabitants of Elis, *Epeioi* (cf. *Iliad* 2.619; 4.537 etc.).

427–29 The identity of Pherai is doubtful. Perhaps this is an alternate spelling for Pharai in Achaia, a town by the river Peiros, half-way between Dymê and Leontion. Doulichion must be modern Leukas and Samê modern Kephallenia. Ithakê and Zakynthos are too well-known to merit comment.

443 These would be votive tripods arranged in rows in front of the temple.

463 Ancient sources give his name as Kastalios or Ikadios.

493–95 The composer of the hymn attributes the cult of Apollon Delphinios to the god's epiphany as a dolphin and seems to be of the opinion that the cult originated in Crete.

Although the name Delphi is not mentioned in the hymn, some modern scholars see the story as a mythological *aition* for the name Delphi and thus also make an etymological connection between *delphis* and Delphi. The Greek form for Delphi is Delphoi, and this form seems to be an old locative of *Delphos. Is it not possible that this word might be related to *delphys* (womb)? Indeed, if Delphi was the *omphalos,* the navel, of the earth, it is not too daring to suggest that in some sense it and its outlying area constituted the womb, and, in a loose sense, the stomach of the earth.

500   Perhaps the *Iēpaiēōn* was a hymn to Apollon the healer (cf. the root *iē*—in *iē-tros* = physician). For the paean, which before the first Sacred War (circa 590 B.C.) was the main event in a musical competition of kithara-players, see Strabo 9.3.12.

518   Cf. *Iliad* 1.472; 22.391.

5-37   The Greeks of historical times—much as they do today about certain monasteries—were in the habit of making unkind remarks about the greed with which the Delphic priests wielded the butcher's knife. The meat, which after all could not all be consumed by the priests, was usually distributed among the inhabitants of Delphi.

39ff.   It is impossible to tell whether line 539 has fallen victim to the ravages of time or a line following it has been altogether lost.

0-44   This is a *vaticinium ex eventu*, a prophecy after the event. There was no Cretan priesthood at Delphi in historical times. The original priests, like many who followed them in the control of the holy precinct, may have been unseated either by the local rivals, who wanted a share of the pie, or by overtaxed pilgrims, who decided that too much was too much.

546   Most of the Homeric Hymns end with this transitional formula.

4. TO HERMES

The *Hymn to Hermes* is somewhat of an oddity among the other hymns. It does not possess any of the depth and the piety that permeate many of the other hymns, and especially the major hymns to Apollon and Demeter. The only other hymn that bears some remote resemblance to it is the *Hymn to Aphrodite,* in which I find a humorous strain, even though milder and rather subdued by comparison. In fact, if it were not for the characteristically Hellenic attitude of mingling humor with piety and the absurd with the profoundly serious, one might be led to consider the *Hymn to Hermes* a spoof or some sort of an early example of mock-epyllion.

In this hymn, Hermes is the trickster and thief par excellence. He is the Loki of the Greek pantheon. That this view was both old and commonly held among the Greeks rather than an innovation by the composer of the hymn is proven by the fact that Homer considered the god a thief and a patron of thieves. In the *Iliad* 24.24 the gods wanted him to go and steal the body of Hector from the plain of Troy where Achilles had been abusing it. In the *Odyssey,* Autolykos, who "surpassed all other men in thievery and perjury," received his dubious talents from Hermes to whom he faithfully sacrificed as his patron (19.395–98). In Hesiod's *Works and Days* we find that it was Hermes who endowed Pandora with a knack for thieving, lying, and wheedling (*Works and Days* 67–68, 77–79). But Hermes was much more than a trickster and a thief. He was a divine herald, a *psychopompos*, that is, he accompanied the souls of the dead to the Underworld, a protector of herds, an inventor—among other things he invented the firedrill and the lyre—a bringer of good luck, a giver of profit, a patron of the wrestling ring, a god of minor divinations by lot, and a protector of the house as Hermes Pylaios. In our hymn there is no indication of his power over the dead, the wrestling ring, or the gates of houses. But all his other powers and qualities are either elaborated or, at least, touched upon.

The poem is a major hymnal composition intended to be comprehensive. That is why the question of unity has plagued its critics. To put it quite simply, how could the rhapsode have given the poem the unity demanded by the modern critics, since he had to compose a poem not about one episode in the life of a god but rather about several episodes in the life of an erratic and elusive god, whose very nature contained inherent contradictions? In fact, the poem has amazing unity. It deals with the accomplishments of a precocious divine baby, who, in a couple of days, invents the lyre and the firedrill, steals the cattle of the gods, becomes skilled in divination, proves Apollon's match in arguing, and wins recognition by Zeus and a place in Olympos for himself and his mother. There is unity of time and unity of theme, the theme being inventiveness and skill in thievery and deception.

The main subject of the hymn, the theft of the divine cattle, may indeed be of old Indo-European stock (in the Vedic parallel Ahi steals the cattle of Indra). Greek literature—one does not know whether by dependence on the hymn or by drawing on common stock—was quite partial to the theft of the divine cattle. Among others Alkaios treated it in a hymn to Hermes. Sophocles dealt with it in the *Ichneutai.* Apollodoros gives his version of it in 3.10.2, and, if we are to judge from Antoninus Liberalis 23, Hesiod, Apollonios Rhodios, and several others tried their hand at it.

The author and the place of composition of the hymn remain unknown. Not much emphasis can be placed on the invention of the seven-stringed lyre as an aid for dating the hymn. This type of lyre was known in Crete in the bronze age, and its introduction to Greece must have been very early. The Triphylian Pylos, which is mentioned in this hymn (342, 355, 398) as the place to which Hermes drove the cattle, was destroyed in the so-called Second Messenian War in the last quarter of the seventh century. Of course, nothing could have prevented a poet of the fifth century from working with an earlier tradition, but chances are that the composition of the hymn antedates the destruction of the Triphylian Pylos and should therefore be placed tentatively somewhere in the middle of the seventh century.

1 Maia, the daughter of Atlas, is important only as the mother of Hermes. Her name means "mother," "nurse," and in the *Odyssey* she is one of the Pleiads (14.435; cf. Hesiod *Theogony* 938).

2 Although several other places claimed to be the birthplace of the god, by and large tradition and literature granted the honor to Mount Kyllene in Arcadia.

15 Surely the reference here is to the Hermai, busts of Hermes on square bases from which an erect phallus projected. They stood at the entrances of private houses and temples in Athens as apotropaic guardians, and the importance attached to them by the Athenians can be gathered from the consternation that followed their mutilation on the eve of the Sicilian expedition in 415 B.C.

19 The division of the month here is bipartite, and this is the first fourth day of the first half of the month. Hesiod reckons (a) simply by days, (b) by a tripartite division into decades, and (c) by a bipartite division into waxing and waning moons. He does not associate the fourth of the month with the birth of Hermes, but he considers it a lucky day (for details see *Works and Days* 765ff.). In classical times the fourth was a lucky day, and both Hermes and Aphrodite were thought to have been born on it.

24 In other sources (Apollodoros 3.10.2, the *Ichneutai* and Eratosthenes *Katasterismoi* 24) the episode of the tortoise follows the theft and slaughter of the cows. This change in the sequence of events must be due to a desire to make it logical: if Hermes slaughtered the cows first, he would have a supply of strings for his lyre.

30–38 The words of Hermes are, of course, ironical, and the passage has a good bit of comic levity with which the entire hymn is permeated. Line 36 is a proverb that occurs in Hesiod *Works and Days* 365. A pun is doubtless intended, since the tortoise, much like the snail, carries its home. For the tortoise as a charm (37), cf. Pliny *Natural History* 32.14. Turtles make little squeaky sounds when they copulate, but are otherwise silent. The idea that the animal was voiceless when alive and "vocal" when dead was comically exploited (cf. *Ichneutai* 292ff.).

47–54 This is the oldest passage on the construction of the lyre for which see Th. Reinach in Daremberg et Saglio 3.1438; Curt Sachs, *The History of Musical Instruments* pp. 129-35, and Bernhard Aign, *Die Geschichte der Musikinstrumente des Ägäischen Raumes bis um 700 vor Christi* (1963), passim through the index. Of the ancient passages *Ichneutai* 302ff., Bion 5.8 and Nicander *Alexipharmaka* 560ff. are most interesting.

54–56 Poetical improvisations of this kind are still performed at folk festivals on the island of Cyprus.

57–67 The transition from singing of the union of Zeus and Maia to conceiving a plan for robbing Apollon of his cattle is abrupt, and perhaps the poet intended to show us that the god's native propensities obsessed him to the point that orderly rational thought yielded to mischievous impulse.

70 Even though there is justified suspicion for thinking that Pieria here has supplanted an earlier *Pêreiê*, for the time being we are forced to be content with identifying this place with the well-known Pieria north of Olympos and Helikon in Macedonia.

71 The reader will remember that in lines 18 and 22 the cattle belong to Apollon. Here we are told that they are property of the gods. In Homer, Apollon does not own cows or oxen. The cattle that were eaten by the men of Odysseus (*Odyssey* 1.8; 12.127ff.) belonged to Helios. Perhaps originally the cattle belonged to Helios, the sun, and then to Apollon-Helios, the sun-god.

77 Horse thieves of my native Epirus employed this ruse to evade their pursuers as late as the early twentieth century. (Cf. Vergil *Aeneid* 8.210; Livy 1.7; *Ichneutai* 110ff.).

88 Onchestos is to the northwest of Thebes.

90 The scene is reminiscent of *Odyssey* 24.227, where Laertes is digging round his vines.

99–100 If the Titan Pallas is meant, he was the son of Krios and Eurybiê (Hesiod *Theogony* 375–76). His brother Persês was the father of Hekate (ibid. 377,409). This might make the Hesiodic Pallas a rather likely candidate for the father of Selene, but Hesiod clearly tells us that Helios and Selene were the children of Hyperion and Theia (ibid. 371–74). Megamedes is otherwise unknown.

102 This is the well-known Alpheios river that flows into the sea near Epitalion, west of Olympia, and on the western shore of the Peloponnese.

108–15 This is the first mention in Greek literature of making fire by means of a drill. (For other accounts cf. Theophrastos in *Peri Phytôn Historias* 5.9.6; the scholiast on Apollonios Rhodios 1.1184 and Pliny *Natural History* 16.8).

124–26 Apollon found the hides when he was searching for his cattle (403–4). The hides that were exhibited to pilgrims could be either natural rocks vaguely suggesting the shape of an oxhide, or stones hewn to that shape by human hand.

128-29 The obvious inference is that the portions correspond to the twelve Olympians, but there are some difficulties in assuming that the number of the Olympians was fixed when this hymn was composed.

127-37 Some scholars have thought that Hermes does not eat the meat that he roasted to conform with the chthonic side of his character. We know that victims were offered to him at Kyllene, and that animal sacrifices to him are attested by Homer (*Odyssey* 14.435; 19.396-98). That Hermes does not eat meat is very strange, since it was a craving for meat that made him steal the cattle. I am afraid that the reason behind this curious behavior will elude us for quite some time.

148 When Pausanias visited the site, the temple of Hermes on top of Kyllene was in ruins (8.17.1). The cave mentioned here has not been identified.

186–87 This is the grove near the temple of Poseidon for which see notes on *Hymn to Apollon* 230–38.

188 "Bulwark of his vineyard" is a parody of the Homeric "bulwark of the Achaians" (of Ajax), "bulwark of Olympos" (of Ares in Hymn 8.3), etc.

216 This is the Triphylian Pylos.

226 The reference is to Hermes' steps. He obviously skidded from one side of the road to the other.

231 The scent emanated from the divine presence. The Greeks still attribute the quality of divine fragrance to many of their saints.

294-98 Sneezing was considered an omen by the ancient Greeks, but the breaking of wind must have been as much a taboo then as it is today. Hermes' behavior is virtually infantile, but the trick proved to be a temporarily effective stratagem. In the *Apocolocyntosis Divi Claudii*, Seneca may indeed have had these lines in mind when he chose Hermes as the divine agent who relieved Claudius of his flatulent travail (*Apocol.* 3).

324 For the "scales of justice" in Homer, cf. *Iliad* 8.69; 16.658; 19.223;22.209.

409 A lacuna is suspected after this line. Some scholars have supposed that Apollon wanted to bind Hermes. In no way can the text yield this meaning. Apollon intended to tie his cattle and bring them back to Pieria. For using withes to tie animals, cf. *Odyssey* 9.427.

415 Another lacuna seems probable here.

26–33 Cf. Hesiod *Theogony* 1–21. For Mnemosyne and her nine daughters, the Muses, see *Theogony* 52–63. Line 430 means that Mnemosyne obtained Hermes by lot, because his musical skill definitely fell within her province.

50–52 Although in the *Hymn to Apollon* 131 Apollon says "may the lyre (kithara) be dear to me . . .," he is not claiming to have invented the instrument. According to Pausanias 9.30.1, Hermes and Apollon contested for the lyre. Nonetheless, the credit for the invention of the lyre incontrovertibly belongs to Hermes.

460 Neither in art nor in literature is Apollon usually depicted as carrying a spear. Here he is justified because he is after the robbers who stole his cattle (cf. *Odyssey* 14.531). In *Iliad* 1.234 Achilles swears by his scepter, that is, by the symbol of his kingly authority. Apollon's oath by the cornel spear, which can hardly be taken as a symbol of his divine power, is in keeping with the comic character of much of this hymn.

80–89 The artistic sensitivity and the truly genteel nature of the advice that Hermes gives Apollon are remarkable. It is small wonder that the best practitioners of the art of singing and playing the lyre were called *theioi* (divine) (so Demodokos in *Odyssey* 8.43, and 47).

508 In many parts of Greece the cults of the two gods were closely connected, and the line is a mere confirmation of a well-known fact.

11–12 Hermes invented the pipe and Pan, his son, became so famous for playing it that many students of the classics commit the venial error of crediting Pan with the invention (cf. Apollodoros 3.10.2).

526 A line is missing after 526.

29–32 Surely the *kêrykeion*, the herald's staff, is meant here. With it, we are told, in both the *Iliad* and the *Odyssey*, the god puts men to sleep and wakes them up (cf. *Iliad* 24.343–44; *Odyssey* 24.1-5). On the other hand, in these lines Apollon gives Hermes the staff as a token of powers far more extensive than we ascribe to the Hermes of classical times.

41–49 Men are to inquire at the oracle only if the omens are auspicious and then only to a point which the god considers proper. This relationship, as well as Apollon's bringing good to some men and harm to others, rests on a justification that is moral only in the etymological sense of the word. Apollon in fact means: "I am the divine law-giver and things are right only so far as they conform to the law as I lay it down; to ask more than that of me is illegal." The muses tell the truth only when they want to (Hesiod *Theogony* 27ff.; Euripides also tells us that it is ignorance to try to force the gods to reveal what they do not wish to [*Ion* 374ff.]).

52–63 The three awesome sisters who fly about like bees and whose heads are besprinkled with white barley flour (cf. the practice of the basket-carrying maidens in Aristophanes' *Ekklesiazousai* 732) must be the Thriai, eponymous nymphs of the *thriai,* that is, of pebbles used for divination (cf. Apollodoros 3.10.2; Cicero *De Divinatione* 1.34). We have no depiction of the Thriai in art and we do not know either how pebbles were used in divination or how the apiform Thriai became mantic after eating honey.

568 There is a lacuna after this line.

569–71 The concept of Hermes as lord of wild beasts is rather extravagant and almost hyperbolic. He had power over domesticated herds and especially sheep, and sacrifices were offered to him so that he might increase the flocks (cf. *Odyssey* 14.435; Hesiod *Theogony* 444–47).

572 Hermes was not simply messenger but also *psychopompos,* "dispatcher of souls" or, more precisely, escort of souls on their journey to the Underworld.

5. TO APHRODITE

The place of composition of this hymn is unknown. Its date seems quite early, somewhere around 700 B.C. The story of the love of Anchises and Aphrodite is at least as old as Homer (*Iliad* 2.819–21 and 5.311–13). Hesiod also knows the story and mentions it briefly in the *Theogony* 1008–10. The brevity of the Homeric and Hesiodic references should not mislead us into thinking that the details of the seduction are altogether new with the poet of the hymn. As we learn from the story of which Demodokos sings in the *Odyssey* (8.266ff.), Aphrodite's amatory escapades caught the fancy of Homer as well. In the above mentioned passages of the *Iliad,* quite simply, Homer felt that at that point in the narrative a digression would be out of place. In later Greek literature Theokritos mentions the episode in 20.34, and Apollodoros gives a somewhat different version in 3.12.2. Given the loveliness of the theme and its possibilities, it is indeed remarkable that it did not become an all time favorite with the Alexandrians and the Romans (cf. however, Propertius 2.32 and 35; Nonnus 15.210).

The lay of Demodokos in the eighth book of the *Odyssey* is patently humorous and racy. The humor of this hymn is subtle and almost reverential. To begin with, the goddess of our hymn has unique powers over beasts, men, and gods. Such are her powers that not even Zeus can escape them. In fact, this one time he takes revenge by "placing in her soul sweet desire to mingle with a mortal" (45). In other words, she is acting under some constraint. This is a superbly playful twist by the poet, who thus prepares the listener for the strangely seductive maidenly coyness of the goddess when she encounters Anchises. She does not appear to him as a *femme fatale* or an overpowering goddess, but rather as a young Phrygian princess who has been abducted by Hermes from among other maidens at a dance in honor of the divine maiden Artemis—the emphasis here is on innocence and virginity—and commanded to become the wife of Anchises. She does not tell him that she is unwilling, but she does tell him that she must comply with dire necessity (130). She also insists—good girl that she is—to meet his parents and his brothers. *La noblesse oblige.* Anchises is not about to be outdone by an ingénue. He can be just as pious to the wishes of the gods. He boasts that neither man nor god—not even Apollon—can prevent him from obeying the command of Hermes! The listener realizes that this is a double put on and cannot but think "Oh, what a way to go!" He undresses her and takes off every last piece of jewelry, as she just stands there with downcast eyes, not lifting a finger to help. Then they lie together, with Anchises still "not knowing clearly" (167). His unclear knowledge does not prevent him from doing his duty and then promptly falling asleep. But Aphrodite is a tease; she cannot wait to break the news to him. So she wakes him up. He gazes upon the goddess as she towers above him in her radiant beauty, and he is seized with surprise and fear for his manhood. The surprise cannot be genuine. After all, he finds out what he already knew, however "unclearly." But the fear is understandable; goddesses have strange ways. However, Aphrodite sooths his anxiety by telling him of the fabulous boy she will bear him and of the fact that there is precedent for what just happened: Zeus took a fancy to Ganymedes and Eos fell in love with Tithonos. The case is even legally justifiable or, at least, sanctioned by precedent. Not only has Anchises not had a bad time of it, but what is more *"non è peccato!"* All this is funny and charming, but it is not impious and picaresque, and this, I think, is to be credited to the unique skill of the composer, who managed to stroll so casually on a veritable literary tightrope.

1   The line is reminiscent of *Odyssey* 1.1. I do not think that the poet has one of the nine Muses in mind, but rather their mother, Mnemosyne, "Memory," whose aid he understandably needs.

2   Aphrodite is called Kypris (and elsewhere Kyprogenês) either because she was born in Cyprus or because she came to it after her birth. The condition of the Hesiodic passage that refers to Aphrodite's birth *(Theogony* 190–206) hardly permits any sort of dogmatic certainty on the subject.

2–6 The power of Aphrodite, as defined by these lines, extends over man and beast and is far greater than the one implied by Hesiod in *Theogony* 205-6, where she presides over "maidenly whispers and smiles and tricks, and over sweet delight and honeylike love." The theme of Aphrodite's power was beautifully elaborated by Lucretius *(De Rerum Natura* 1-49), for whom the goddess is not essentially only the divine muse invoked to help him in his great undertaking but also the deity governing the *natura rerum* (21). Hesiod tells us that Aphrodite was called Kythereia because, as she was floating on the sea, she came close to Kythera, the little island off the coast of the Southern Peloponnese *(Theogony* 198).

7–32 This excursus on the chaste character of Athena, Artemis, and Hestia is not only in keeping with the leisurely and digressive pace of the epic but also constitutes a clever foil that brings Aphrodite's amatory nature out into full relief.

8–11   Nilsson's theory (in *Anfänge der Göttin Athene*, 1921) that Athena originally was the warlike patroness and palace goddess of the Mycenaean kings is very probable. Her masculine character is also shown by the fact that she was born from the head of Zeus (for Hera's anger, see *Hymn to Apollon* 305–362). Behind Athena's aversion to the whole domain of Aphrodite's power may be the justifiable suspicion of men, that sexual love enfeebles men and deprives them of such manly qualities as the warrior can ill afford to lose.

12–15   Athena was the patroness of crafts and of women's handiwork. In *Odyssey* 6.233 we find her as patron goddess of goldsmiths, and in Athens the smiths held a festival (the *Chalkeia*) in her honor. The epithet *Erganê*, the "Work-woman" also attests to her connection with craft and handiwork. Hesiod (*Works and Days* 430) calls the plough-builder servant of Athena.

16–20   See notes on *Hymn to Artemis* (27).

21–32   Hestia was the first child born to Rhea and Kronos; Demeter was second, and Hera third (Hesiod *Theogony* 454). As the oldest child, Hestia was first to be swallowed and last to be disgorged by her father (*Theogony* 495ff.). Thus, in a sense she was also the youngest. She was the first and last deity to whom libations were poured at a feast. Mythology never made much of Apollon's and Poseidon's wooing of Hestia, perhaps because she never became truly anthropomorphic. Furthermore, whenever she was thought of in human form, she was considered a virgin. This last concept of the goddess as a virgin is also supported by the fact that the priestesses of her etymologically cognate divine counterpart in Rome, Vesta, had to remain chaste during their service to the temple. Line 30 is consonant with Homeric practice, since the hearth was in the center of the *megaron*. The claim that Hestia "for all mortals is of all the gods the most venerated" (32) needs some qualification. Surely Hestia was not more venerated than Zeus. The poet must mean that, where life from day to day was concerned, much of the domestic piety was lavished on Hestia, who presided over the lares and penates of the pagan household. Hesiod has only one curious injunction with regard to Hestia: a man should avoid showing his genitals to Hestia if they are besprinkled with semen (*Works and Days* 733-34). The virginal nature of the goddess may have been the reason why such unsightly testimony of copulation might be repugnant to her and therefore offensive.

34–35   Cf. Sophocles *Antigone* 788-90, Euripides *Hippolytos* 1264–75.

36–52   For Zeus' susceptibility to Aphrodite's power and his impressive extramarital adventures, see Hesiod *Theogony* 886ff. Zeus' own immodest account is found in *Iliad* 14.312ff.

60–64   Here the Graces (Charites) are attendants of Aphrodite. In the *Iliad*, Diomedes pierces with his spear Aphrodite's robe, which was the work of the Graces (5.334–39). For the close connection between the Graces and Aphrodite see Pausanias 6.24.7.

70-74   Wild beasts fawn on Odysseus' men as they approach the palace of Kirke (*Odyssey*
11-19).   For wild animals fawning on approaching goddesses see Apollonios
Rhodios 1.1144; 3.878; 4.672. For Aphrodite's effect on the animal kingdom see
Lucretius' highly poetical account in *De Rerum Natura* 10–20.

81-85   The idea here is that however much a goddess may change, she is still divine enough to
look extraordinary. Thus, in the *Hymn to Demeter* even though the goddess is disguised
as an old woman, when she enters the palace of Keleos her head touches the roof-beam
and the doors are filled with divine radiance (184-86). Yet, no one recognizes her
because "gods are not easily seen by men" (111).

02-106   Anchises is far more perceptive than the womenfolk at the palace of Keleos; he knows
that Aphrodite is a goddess.

1-112   We may conjecture that this is the same Otreus, who, in the *Iliad,* together with Mygdon,
is king of the Phrygians (3.182–90).

13-116   This is the first passage in which the difference between the language of the Trojans and
the Phrygians is recognized. Homer made no attempt to present the speech of the
non-Greeks of his epics in such a way as to show us that they were speakers of foreign
languages. Yet he knew that languages other than Greek were spoken by the Asians of
the Trojan host (*Iliad* 2.808; 4.437) and that the Carians were "barbarophone."

17-125   Although Aphrodite lies, she is still anxious to tell Anchises that she is a princess and
that she is admitted to the company of nymphs. The very fact that she is part of a
divine scheme is proof of considerable importance.

26-142   Aphrodite's plea is both ingenious and ingenuous. She offers herself to Anchises in
marriage as a nobly dowered young bride, who wants all proprieties observed and who
does this out of pious compliance with divine will. Her attitude mirrors the typically
Greek attitude expressed in the phrase *theós pou,* "somehow a god (did it)."

45-154   Anchises' answer is rather humorous, since he really turns compelling necessity to
virtue and piety. In truth he is so inflamed by the beauty of the young girl that he is
willing to defy the arrows of Apollon and even to die for the pleasure of going to bed
with her (for the irrational passion that Aphrodite can inspire cf. *Odyssey* 8.335–42).

51-165   An inferior poet would have Aphrodite undress herself. But we must remember that
she is a coy and untouched young maiden, whose feigned passivity emboldens the
resolve of the young shepherd to take her maidenhood.

72-175   The lines are reminiscent of the *Hymn to Demeter* 188-90.

80-190   There is a modern Greek proverb, "Who saw God and did not fear him?"—we might
think that it is this general apprehension in the presence of the divine that seizes
Anchises. But Anchises has not simply seen Aphrodite; he has lain with her. In modern
Greek folklore men who have been seduced into intercourse with a Nereid usually lose
their wits and betimes their manhood. In the epic of Gilgamesh the hero rejects the
advances made by Ishtar because he knows that the lovers of this Eastern Aphrodite
come to no good end. Kalypso does not harm Odysseus, but obviously Kirke has the
power to deprive Odysseus of his manliness (*Odyssey* 10.301). Perhaps Anchises fears

95

that, once the goddess has taken her pleasure with him, she will make him impotent to make sure that no mortal woman can ever boast of having lain with the favorite of Aphrodite.

196–99 The poet derives the name from *ainós* (dread, awesome) and adds the usual folk etymology. In the *Iliad,* Aineias is one of the foremost and bravest Trojan leaders, frequently mentioned side by side with Hector (17.513).

202–17 In the *Iliad* it is the other gods and not Zeus himself who abduct Ganymedes (20.230–35). For the fabulous horses of Tros see *Iliad* 5.265–72.

218–38 Here the myth of Eos and Tithonos is fully developed. Homer knows Tithonos as a consort of Eos but mentions nothing about Eos' thoughtless request that reduced her lover to such unending misery (cf. *Iliad* 20.237; 11.1). Sappho (58 LP; appendix 118 Loeb) and Mimnermos (12 West) follow the tradition of the Homeric Hymn. The story that Tithonos was eventually turned into a cicada is much later.

260 Nymphs lived long but were not immortal.

262 Seilenoi are often portrayed as lovers of nymphs on Greek vases.

264–72 This belief must go back to an even more primitive animistic concept according to which the tree was hardly distinguished from its spirit. Later the spirit detached itself, became anthropomorphic, and lived an existence which was independent as long as the tree lived, but came to an end when the tree died (cf. Pindar fr. 61; Kallimachos *Hymn 4 To Delos* 83–85; Ovid *Metamorphoses* 8.738–878).

276–78 Herodotos tells us that Persian children were not seen by their fathers before the age of five, and that up to that time they passed their time in the company of women (1.136).

6. TO APHRODITE

The date and place of composition for this shorter hymn to Aphrodite are unknown. The hymn may not be very late, but it is not very early either. The poet may have been a Cypriot.

1–5 In Homer, Aphrodite is the daughter of Zeus and Dionê (*Iliad* 5.312). The poet of this hymn obviously follows Hesiod's account, who has Aphrodite born in the sea from the foam that surrounded the genitals of Ouranos. In fact, Hesiod believes that the name of the goddess is derived from the *aphros,* the "foam" in which she was nourished (*Theogony* 173–206).

5–14 The Horae and the Graces (Charites) are almost identical. In Hesiod the Horae collaborate with the Graces to adorn and deck out Pandora (*Works and Days* 69–82). According to Hesiod they are three in number, *Eunomia, Dikê,* and *Eirenê* (*Theogony* 900). In Attica, too, their number was three (*Thallô, Karpô, Auxô*), but in Hellenistic times they were identified with the four seasons. The vacillation in classical art between two and three Horae may mirror the Indo-European concept of the year as divided into a cold and warm period (winter-summer) as well as into three distinct seasons, winter, spring, and summer.

7. TO DIONYSOS

Some scholars have seen less skill and grace in this hymn, and they have tried to place it either in Alexandrian times or, worse yet, within our own era. Others have found a dithyrambic quality in it. I take this to mean that they have felt some resemblance between this hymn and the dithyrambic poems by Bacchylides. These assumptions are erroneous, especially as they fail to appreciate the fact that there is not one single thing in this hymn that bespeaks either artlessness or a late date. Further, our knowledge of dithyrambic poetry is so meagre that it is rather otiose to venture into any comparisons. The hymn treats an episode out of the god's life and evolves along the lines of a reasonably common thematic motif, which is based on the idea that most men are blind to the presence of divinity, and that gods are forced to resort to thaumaturgy in order to manifest their divine nature. I suppose it is the quick and almost cinematic pace of the poet that has caught critics by surprise. Digression and formulaic repetition are absent. But the poet should not be castigated for his economy of literary devices. He has a moral to teach, and he does it by painting a very lovely and telling picture with a few slightly nervous but powerful strokes. As for the date, there is no good reason to believe that the hymn is later than the sixth century.

1 See note 4 on the *Fragments of the Hymn to Dionysos* (1).

2ff. The story of the capture of Dionysos by pirates is found in several other literary sources: Euripides *Cyclops* 11ff.; Apollodoros 3.5.3; Ovid *Metamorphoses* 3.582–691; Hyginus *Fabula* 134; and so forth. A modified version of the story forms the theme on the choregic monument of Lysikrates (334 B.C.).

3-6 Except for the cloak on his shoulders, the youthful Dionysos resembles an archaic Greek *kouros* and is very different from the blond, curly-haired and seductive Dionysos of Euripides' *Bacchae* 233-41. The Aristophanic caricature of the god in the *Frogs* is also a far cry from the robust and virile youth of our hymn.

8 There are other stories in which the Tyrsenians are pirates (cf. the story of the rape of the Athenian women at Brauron in Herodotos 6. 138). Although writers of the fifth century B.C. used the names Tyrsenians and Pelasgians to refer to the pre-Hellenic world, there is nothing eliminating the possibility that the composer of the hymn might have the better-known Etruscans (also called Tyrsenians) in mind, whose piratic raids must have been familiar to the Greeks in early historic times.

13 Cf. Euripides *Bacchae* 447, 498, 616ff.

19-20 The point is that Dionysos looks like a god. He certainly does not look like fair-haired Apollon or like the bearded Zeus and Poseidon, but gods frequently changed their form, and, in addition to this, the helmsman's awe would make attention to such obvious differences less effective.

29 The Hyperboreans were a northerly legendary folk visited by Apollon part of the year. Homer does not know of them, and they occur first in Hesiod *Fr.* 209 (cf. Alkaios A.I(c) LP,1.1 Loeb; Pindar *Olympian Ode* 3; Herodotos 4.32).

35–44 These lines are reminiscent of the famous vase of Exekias, now one of the prize possessions of the *Antike Kunstsammlung* in Munich.

44 Dionysos is frequently transformed into a lion (cf. Euripides *Bacchae*).

53 In the Exekias vase Dionysos is represented as a bearded regal man, majestically reclining in a boat from whose mast and rigging vine branches and grapes are hanging. Dolphins swim about the boat. Although it cannot be maintained that these dolphins are the transformed pirates of our story here, a conflation of motifs is by no means impossible.

8. TO ARES

Both the accumulation of epithets in the beginning and the astrological character of the hymn make it more than probable that we are dealing with a late—perhaps Alexandrian or even later—poem. So odd seems the inclusion of this poem among the Homeric Hymns that scholars are at a loss for an explanation.

4 Nikê (Victory) is the daughter of Styx and Pallas (Hesiod *Theogony* 383–84). Ares begets Victory only in a symbolic manner. Themis is a Titan and the daughter of Ouranos and Gaia (*Theogony* 135). She is also Zeus' second consort, and as such she gives birth to the Horai and Moirai. Since her name means "established custom," "law." "justice," she eventually becomes an abstraction. Here "succorer of Themis" surely means "succorer of Justice."

5 In Greek the words *kakos* (bad, cowardly) and *kalos* (noble, brave) are antonyms. Since the antonym of bad is good, Ares, who is patron of the "good" is perforce patron and leader of the just. In cult Ares was not linked with the concept of justice or law, and in the *Iliad* there is no sentiment that the god of war chooses to fight on the side of the just. The ultimate meaning of the line must be that those who support law and order may resort to war, hoping to enlist the support of Ares, who, as a god, should be expected to refuse his support to the lawless and the unruly. After all, in Homer kingly authority comes from Zeus, and Ares should come to the aid of the side favored by his father.

6–8 Here the poet switches from Ares the god to Ares the planet (Mars). The peculiar redness of Mars was known to the ancients, and astronomical literature refers to the planet with several adjectives that contain the word *pyr* (fire) as their base. Ares is carried "above the third heavenly arch" because in all Greek astronomical systems he occupied the third planetary zone, counting from the one farthest from the earth (counting from the one closest to the earth, his zone was fifth).

9–15 Although general astrological doctrine taught that the influence of Mars was untoward and evil, I very much doubt that this line is euphemistic. The composer of the hymn does not distinguish between Ares the god and Ares the planet. He bypasses astrological doctrine and dwells on those qualities of the god that are potentially positive.

16 Since Ares controls war, he also controls peace (cf. *Orphic Hymn* 65.6).

9. TO ARTEMIS

There should be little doubt as to the place of origin of the hymn. It must be Asia Minor rather than the Aegaean or mainland Greece. The date need not be late.

3 Although in art and literature Artemis is sometimes connected with horses, it is usually stags and deer that she drives (so on the frieze of Apollon's temple at Bassai). The river Meles flowed near Smyrna, and according to one story Homer was born on its banks and composed his poems in a nearby grotto (Paus. 7.5.6.). The river is represented on coins of Smyrna.

4 Smyrna is mentioned because the goddess would naturally pay a quick visit to her temple there (cf. Quintus Smyrnaeus 7.310).

5 For Klaros see note on *Hymn to Apollon* (3. 30–44).

10. TO APHRODITE

This brief prelude may have been composed by a patriotic Cypriot. Its brevity does not allow us to make any safe pronouncements on its date.

1 Cf. Hesiod *Theogony* 196–99.

2 Cf. Hesiod *Theogony* 206 and Mimnermos 1.3 West.

3 Cf. Sappho 1.13–14 LP and Loeb.

11. TO ATHENA

This brief hymn has the basic characteristics of a prelude, and it may be quite early.

Athena is called "defender of cities" in *Iliad* 6.305. Her usual title is *poliouchos*, "holder or keeper of cities." Although Athena and Ares were rarely worshipped or invoked together, instances to the contrary are not wanting (cf. Paus. 5.15.6 and 1.8.5; also Pindar *Nemean Ode* 10.84).

Athena does not only protect cities under siege, but she also "sacks" cities. Her role as defender of cities was taken over by the Holy Virgin, who in the famous hymn (to be precise, it is a *kontakion*) of the Greek Orthodox Church composed by Romanos Melodos in Constantinople after the "rebellion of Nika" in 532, is called "defending general."

99

12. TO HERA

As there is no farewell to the deity addressed—and this, incidentally, is the only example of its kind in the entire collection—these lines may be just the introduction to a longer poem.

In Hesiod's *Theogony* 11, Hera "walks in golden sandals" and in *Theogony* 433–34 we are told that "golden-sandaled" Hera is the daughter of Kronos and Rhea. Cf. also *poikilothronos* (of the intricate or variegated throne), said of Aphrodite in Sappho 1.1.

13. TO DEMETER

This is merely a combination of the formulae of address and farewell and most certainly not a cento from the longer hymn to Demeter.

See notes on the longer hymn to Demeter (2).

14. TO THE MOTHER OF THE GODS

Although it is quite plausible that the hymn was composed as a prelude to recitation at some sort of orgiastic worship, there is no indication that it is Orphic or late. In fact, its stark directness and lack of mythological elaboration make it definitely pre-Alexandrian.

1–2 The "Mother of the Gods" is frequently identified with Rhea, as for example in *Orphic Hymn* 14 (cf. *Orphic Hymn* 27), where she is simply called "Mother of the Gods"). That Rhea is thought of as Mother of the Gods is clear from *Iliad* 15.187 and Hesiod's *Theogony* 453, 625, and 634. By "Muse" the poet may have meant either all of the Muses collectively or just one, perhaps, Kalliope (cf. Hesiod *Theogony*, 1–115).

3 The line reminds us of the worship of Kybele.

4 The lion is the Mother's most devoted companion in poetry, vase painting, and sculpture.

15. TO LION-HEARTED HERAKLES

So Panhellenic was the worship of Herakles that there is no good reason to ascribe the hymn to a Theban rhapsode. It is pre-Alexandrian and may be as early as the sixth century.

1–3 For the circumstances of the birth of Herakles see Hesiod *Shield*, 1–54.

4–8 Cf. Hesiod *Theogony* 950–55; Pindar *Nemean Ode* 1.72 and 10.17, *Isthmian Ode* 4.65.

9 The phrase that I have translated "Grant me virtue and happiness" is both conventional and formulaic. However, to pray to Herakles for virtue, especially manly virtue which

is most likely meant here, is appropriate. Although *olbos* (happiness) may also mean "wealth," and although among the Greeks of Southern Italy Herakles was connected with commerce, in my opinion one should cautiously refrain from taking the formula too literally.

16.   TO ASKLEPIOS

In the *Iliad,* Asklepios is called a "blameless physician" (11.518). The two physicians of the Greeks at Troy, Machaon and Podaleirios, are his sons (2.732). Although his worship spread far and wide in the Hellenic world, it seems to have originated in Thessalian Trikka. In Hellenistic times Epidauros and Kos boasted the most splendid temples to Asklepios. Originally, Asklepios must have been a hero-physician, who was eventually elevated to divine status. The present hymn does not emphasize the Thessalian origin. As for the date, the sixth century is a good guess.

1–5   For the story of the birth of Asklepios, see Hesiod *Fr.* 58, Pindar. *Pythian Ode* 3; Ovid *Metamorphoses* 2.600–634.

17.   TO THE DIOSKOUROI

See the notes on the longer *Hymn to the Dioskouroi* (33.)

18.   TO HERMES

12   The word that I have translated "giver of things graceful" is *charidôtês,* which more literally means "giver of grace" (cf. *Odyssey* 15.319–20). For a cult of *Hermes Charidôtês* see Plutarch *Moralia* 503 (*Quaestiones Graecae*). Some of the notes on the longer *Hymn to Hermes* (4) are also applicable to this shorter version. Hymn 18 seems to be an abstraction of 4 and as such a more convenient prelude than 4, which is too long to be easily used as a mere introduction. Both hymns may be from the same century.

19.   TO PAN

Art and literature before the sixth century B.C. take little or no notice of Pan. Indeed, in the first half of the millennium Pan seems to have remained a wantonly sportive and gamboling god of the Arcadian woodlands. Before 490 B.C. there was no shrine of Pan in Athens, and it seems that his cult was introduced as a result of his decisive intervention in behalf of the Athenians in the struggle against the Persians (Herodotos 6.105). It is highly unlikely that the hymn antedates the battle of Marathon (490) and equally unlikely that it is Alexandrian. The fifth century seems a reasonable date and Attica a probable place of composition.

2   These epithets are well attested in literature and art.

3–7   The domain of Pan was in the hills of Arcadia, among which Lykaion, Kyllene, Mainalos and Parthenion were especially sacred to him.

12–16   Much as Artemis, the goddess of woodland and beast, goat-footed Pan is both a hunter and a patron of hunters. One of the scholia on Theocritos 7.106 tells us that Arcadian boys struck images of Pan with squills whenever hunting was not successful.

17–18   The bird, of course, is the nightingale, and the lines are vaguely reminiscent of Sophocles' *Oedipus Coloneus* 670–79.

19–24   For Pan and the nymphs see W. H. Roscher, *Lexikon* 3.1390 and 1420.

22–26   Pan's reputation as a dancer is commonplace in classical literature (cf. Pindar fr. 85–90; Sophocles *Ajax* 696; Aeschylus *Persians* 450).

31   Cf. *Hymn to Hermes* (4.1–9).

34   The nymph in question is Dryope, daughter of Dryops, and originally perhaps an oak spirit.

35–39   For another version of the story of Dryope, cf. Stephanus Byzantinus *sub* Dryope and Ovid *Metamorphoses* 9.325ff.

42   Coins from Messana and Rhegium show the hare as a symbol of Pan.

46   On the connection between Pan and Dionysos cf. Lucian *Dialogue of the Gods* 22.3.

47   This is good folk etymology. The root *pa* seen in the Greek **paomai* (to acquire) and Latin *pascor* (feed, graze on) is a more likely linguistic ancestor of Pan.

20.   TO HEPHAISTOS

1–8   The concept of Hephaistos and Athena as joint patrons of handicraft is found in Homer (*Odyssey* 6.233). It is interesting that it is Hephaistos who, at the behest of Zeus, creates Pandora out of earth and water, and that Athena teaches her the art of weaving (Hesiod *Works and Days* 59–64). Although there are indications that Hephaistos was worshipped in other parts of the Hellenic world, Athens and Lemnos were the two most prominent centers of his worship. In connection with the Lemnian cult of Hephaistos, about which we know very little, it is interesting to speculate that it must have been old. In the *Iliad* we are told that, when the angered Zeus casts Hephaistos out of the divine threshold, Hephaistos, after a full day's journey through the air, lands on Lemnos, where the legendary Sinties look after him (*Iliad* 1.586–94). In Athens, Hephaistos and Athena were worshipped together as patrons of arts and crafts (cf. Plato *Kritias* 109c, 112b; *Laws* 920d; *Protagoras* 321d). For their place in Orphic belief see Fragments 178, 179 Kern. As with the preceding hymn, Athens and the fifth century seem to be the probable place and date of composition.

21. TO APOLLON

This hymn is not a cento and does not stand in a derivative relationship to Hymn 3. It is a clever rhapsodic prelude of unknown date and place of composition.

1-2 Peculiar though it may seem to us, the ancients believed that a musical sound was produced by the flapping of the swan's wings (cf. Anacreontea 60.10 Bergk PLG).

3 Peneios is the lovely Thessalian river that flows into the Thermaic gulf.

4 Hesiod is commanded to sing of the Muses first and last *(Theogony* 34).

22. TO POSEIDON

Although the hymn seems like a short prayer to the god of the sea, there is no formal criterion that separates it from the shorter preludes. Date and place of composition are unknown.

2 The line is addressed to Poseidon as god of earthquakes and of the sea. In the Homeric epics Poseidon is called *enosichthôn* (Earth-Shaker) in numerous passages, but he considered himself *homotimos* (of equal honor) to Zeus and Hades, because when the tripartite division was made, he was given the sea as his realm (*Iliad* 15.186-91).

3 There is surely a connection between the assertion made in this line and the cult epithet *Helikônios* under which Poseidon was worshipped by the various Ionian states. Despite the geographical proximity of Helike to Aigai—both were situated on the Corinthian gulf—and the fact that both are mentioned in the *Iliad* as sacred to Poseidon (8.203), the attempts to derive the title *Helikônios* from Helike rather than from Helikon are linguistically unsound.

5 For Poseidon as an instructor in horsemanship and a tamer of horses see *Iliad* 23.307; Sophocles *Oedipus Coloneus* 712-15; Aristophanes *Knights* 551-58. His function as savior of ships, usually more appropriate to the Dioskouroi (cf. *Hymn* 33), in modern times has been taken over by Saint Nikolaos.

23. TO ZEUS

It is peculiar that Zeus, the chief of the gods, is hymned only in this rather unpretentious prelude that he shares with Themis. One wonders whether the father of the gods was felt to be somewhat remote and inaccessible. It is quite interesting that in Greek Orthodoxy, although many benedictions and tropes begin with the phrase "in the name of the Father . . . ," it is Jesus, Mary, and the Saints who are the hymnists' favorites. Date and place of composition are unknown.

1-4 Zeus is invoked as counselor and law-giver. This is clearly implied by the presence of Themis, whose legalistic and pacific nature is betrayed by her daughters Eunomia

(Good-Law), Dikê (Justice) and Eirenê (Peace) concerning whom see Hesiod *Theogony* 901–6. Although, as this Hesiodic passage attests, Themis was Zeus' second wife, here she seems to be more of a *paredros*, a "coadjutor." For Themis in Homer see *Iliad* 15.87–100; 20.4–6; *Odyssey* 2.68–9.

24.   TO HESTIA

Although Hestia was never completely personified, here she is definitely invoked as an anthropomorphic goddess. Originally she was simply the hearth and the fire that burned in the hearth. She was both a familial and a civic deity, since public buildings also contained a hearth on which the well-being of the city depended, much as the well-being of the family depended on the hearth of its dwelling. The hymn does not seem to be earlier than the fifth century B.C.

1–2   The reference is to the sacred hearth at Delphi.

  3   Sacrificial oil was frequently poured on sacred stones and on the heads of the divine statues.

  4   The occasion seems to be the construction of a new dwelling and not, as some scholars think, of a temple.

  5   It was not uncommon to invoke Hestia together with Zeus; in Homer the hearth is invoked along with Zeus (*Odyssey* 14.158-59), and in time the two deities merged in the concept of *Zeus Ephestios*, "Zeus of the Hearth." However, our line is still puzzling, because one does not think of gods of the hearth as particularly connected with the grace of song.

25.   TO THE MUSES AND APOLLON

1–7   In the *Iliad* the Muses sing as Apollon plays the lyre (1.601–4). The Iliadic scene is not substantially different from *Hymn 3* (*To Apollon*) 189–93 (cf. also *Hymn 4 To Hermes* 450–52). The invocation of Zeus, who is father of both Apollon and of the Muses, is quite natural. Equally natural is the joint worship of Apollon and the Muses, because he played the lyre and they usually sang. Our poet's invocation is most appropriate, since he presumably is both a lyre player and a singer. Most commentators consider this poem a cento from Hesiod's *Theogony* 1–104 (specifically, lines 2–5 from *Theogony* 94–97, and line 6 from *Theogony* 104). This hymn may be as early as the late seventh or, more probably, the sixth century.

26.   TO DIONYSOS

Despite its brevity, this piece has an honest exuberance such as one might expect of a song sung at a Dionysiac festival. The date may be rather early. See notes to Hymns 1 and 7.

27. TO ARTEMIS

The hymn is simple and charming. Artemis is depicted as a youthful huntress who comes to Delphi to lead the Muses and the Graces in the dance. In the earlier stage of the cult of Apollon at Delphi, Artemis was of little or no importance, but in classical times she was introduced into the cult and even shared some of Apollon's cult epithets (e.g., *Delphinia, Pythia*). We know that hymns such as this were recited at Delphi on certain festive occasions, and it is quite possible that our hymn was composed for one of these. Comparison with the long hymn to Apollon shows that the composer of this short hymn to Artemis may have consciously borrowed from the song in honor of the Delphic god. The piece is charming but not precious, and it may have been composed before the fifth century B.C.

28. TO ATHENA

Even though there is nothing in the poem betraying the place of its origin, Attica and especially Athens would be a good guess, because at no other place was Athena honored as much. In fact, the Panathenaic festival would have been a most fitting occasion for the composition of such a hymn. The date may well be the fifth century.

3 Cf. Hymn 11 (*To Athena*).
4 The cult epithet *Tritogeneia* is of unknown origin and meaning.
4-12 Cf. the Hesiodic account in *Theogony* 886-900; see also Pindar *Olympian Ode* 7.35-44.

29. TO HESTIA

1-6 See Notes on *Hymn* 24 and especially notes on lines 21-32 of *Hymn* 5 (*To Aphrodite*).
6-14 This joint invocation to Hestia and Hermes may at first appear strange. The reader will readily recall Hermes as messenger of the gods or as *psychopompos,* but not as a tutelary household deity. It should be said, however, that this hymn, much like *Hymn* 24, was composed for the occasion of the solemn consecration of a new dwelling. Hermes' phallic statue stood outside the Athenian house, and in this role the god was not only apotropaic but also surely acted as a protector of the family's fertility. Further, Hermes was a bringer of good luck, and that is exactly what a new home needs. It is a combination of these roles that makes Hermes not a strange but in fact a most natural companion of Hestia for the occasion that we assume as the reason for the poem. There is no clue as to the date and place of composition.

30. TO EARTH, MOTHER OF ALL

That there should be echoes from the *Hymn to Demeter* in this poem is quite natural. After all, Demeter-Rhea-Kybele-Earth, Mother of All-the Mother of the Gods are nothing less than different versions of the primeval womb, the archetypal mother, who has given birth to everything that lives. Although it is not clear on what occasion such a poem might have been recited or sung, it is a true *prooimion*. Its date of composition may fall anywhere within the fifth or fourth centuries.

1–19   The reader should compare the hymn with *Orphic Hymn* 26. However, there is nothing that makes *Hymn* 30 especially Orphic. It is interesting to note that it is not clear whether the poet conceived of Gaia as anthropomorphic. He rightly calls her "mother of all and oldest of all," because Chaos, which preceded her, was in essence the Void into which she was born. Ouranos (sky), to whom the generation of all subsequent Greek gods is to be traced, was her child, and it was in incestuous union with him that she gave birth to Kronos (see Hesiod *Theogony* 116ff.).

31. TO HELIOS

The reader should compare the hymn with *Orphic Hymn* 8. Although Helios (sun) was invoked in oaths, Rhodes was the only place in which he played an important role in public cult. There is no hint as to the date and place of composition for either Hymn 31 or 32.

1   The customary invocation was to a Muse or goddess, but Alcman too names Kalliope (27 PMG, 43 Loeb). It was in later times, Roman in fact, that the Muses were differentiated according to their various functions. Kalliope became traditionally the Muse of heroic epic.

2–7   Euryphaëssa occurs only here. In Hesiod *Theogony* 371–74, it is Theia who gives birth to Helios, Selene (moon) and Eos (dawn).

8–16   In the hands of later poetasters the image of Helios on his horses or on a chariot drawn by horses became virtually hackneyed (cf. Seneca *Apocolocyntosis* 2). The concept is not Homeric, but common in the hymns (2.63 and 88; 4.69; 28.14).

32. TO SELENE

2   "Long-winged Moon" is an oddity, which may have arisen from confusing Selene with Eos.

11   Cf. Pindar *Olympian Ode* 3.19.

14   This love affair of Zeus with Selene is not mentioned in the catalogue of his amorous accomplishments in the *Theogony* 886ff.

15   Pandeia's name can be connected with the adjective *pandios* (all-luminous) with reasonable certainty. The daughter is an extension and abstraction of the mother. Connection with the Athenian festival of Pandia has not been definitely established.

33. TO THE DIOSKOUROI

There is a good chance that this hymn is much older than *Hymn* 17, and that in fact it may antedate the sixth century B.C. Stylistic grounds have led scholars to link this hymn with the one to Dionysos (7) and to feel that Theokritos imitated it in *Idyll* 22.

1–3 In the *Iliad,* Kastor, the tamer of horses and Polydeukes, the boxer, are not divine. They are sons of Tyndareus and mortal heroes whom Priam, not knowing that they are dead and buried in Lacedemon, expects to see among the other heroes in Troy (*Iliad* 3.236–45). In the *Odyssey* this same tradition is accepted, but it is added that "Life-giving earth holds them alive;/and honored by Zeus even below the earth/they take turns in living and dying on alternate days./Their honor is equal to that of the gods" (*Odyssey* 11.301–4). The tradition that makes Zeus the father of Kastor and Polydeukes is therefore post-Homeric, and its earliest occurrence must be Hesiod's *Ehoiai* (66 Loeb). The patronymic Tyndaridai refers to their putative father, and it was used both in literature and cult. Interestingly enough, there is no trace in this hymn of Leda's seduction by Zeus, in the form of a swan. According to the older tradition only Helen was born of that peculiar union (Euripides *Helena* 16–22). It was obviously the Alexandrian mythographers who had the divine twins hatched out of the swan's egg.

5 Lakonia was the center from which the worship of the Dioskouroi spread to other parts of Greece.

6–19 It is quite possible that it was their role in the Argonautic saga that secured the heroic twins their thaumaturgic role as saviors of imperiled sailors. Their epiphany usually took the form of twin lights of St. Elmo's fires. This identification eventually led to astral connections, especially with the constellation of the Gemini. Interesting speculations have been made about the relationship of Kastor and Polydeukes to the Aśvin, the divine horse-riding twins of Sanskrit mythology, but nothing conclusive has been proven.

TO GUEST-FRIENDS

M, of course, does not contain this piece, which is included in manuscripts of the *X* family and in manuscripts *C,D.* The version of the hymn corpus and that of the *Vita Herodotea* show great textual divergence.

It is absurd to translate the title *To Strangers,* especially in view of the first line of the poem where the word *xénia,* "gifts of guest-friendship," clearly defines the meaning of the title. The fact that the poem is in the *Vita Herodotea* (c. 200 A.D.) does not indicate that it was transferred from it to the corpus of the hymns. Its date is unknown, and it seems to be of Aeolic, or, at least, Chian origin. The piece has been taken as an *envoi* by the poet of the hymns to the inhabitants of Aeolic Kymê, by the river Hermos.